Social Security Act

LANDMARK LEGISLATION
Social Security Act

Clifton Park - Halfmoon Public Library
475 Moe Road
Clifton Park, New York 12065

Richard Worth

mc Marshall Cavendish
Benchmark
New York

With thanks to Catherine McGlone, Esq., for her expert review of this manuscript.

Other Marshall Cavendish Offices:
Marshall Cavendish International (Asia) Private Limited, 1 New Industrial Road, Singapore 536196 • Marshall Cavendish International (Thailand) Co. Ltd., 253 Asoke, 12th Flr, Sukhumvit 21 Road, Klongtoey Nua, Wattana, Bangkok 10110, Thailand • Marshall Cavendish (Malaysia) Sdn Bhd, Times Subang, Lot 46, Subang Hi-Tech Industrial Park, Batu Tiga, 40000 Shah Alam, Selangor Darul Ehsan, Malaysia
Marshall Cavendish is a trademark of Times Publishing Limited.

All websites were available and accurate when this book was sent to press.

"From Bill to Law" is used by permission of Susan Dudley Gold.

Library of Congress Cataloging-in-Publication Data
Worth, Richard.
Social Security Act / by Richard Worth.
p. cm. — (Landmark legislation)
Includes bibliographical references and index.
ISBN 978-1-60870-043-1
1. Social security—Law and legislation—United States—Juvenile literature. 2. Social security—Law and legislation—United States—History—20th century—Juvenile literature. I. Title.
KF3650.W67 2011
344.7302'3—dc22
2009032233

Publisher: Michelle Bisson
Art Director: Anahid Hamparian
Series Designer: Sonia Chaghatzbanian
Photo research by Candlepants, Inc.

Cover photo: President Franklin D. Roosevelt signs the Social Security Act into law.

The photographs in this book are used by permission and through the courtesy of: Corbis/Bettmann: cover; AP Images: 2, 32, 41, 49; Al Goldis: 80; Pat Sullivan: 91; Mark Humphrey: 94; Eric Risberg, 98; David Lienemann: 105; Getty Images/Mike Simons: 3, 67; Mark Wilson: 6; Paul Briol/Cincinnati Museum Center: 10; MPI: 13; Russell Lee: 16; Transcendental Graphics: 27; Ben Shahn/Library of Congress: 29; George Skadding/Time Life Pictures: 44; Frank Culbertson/Courtesy of NASA: 58; The Granger Collection: 20; Corbis/Bettmann: 36, 53; Franklin Delano Roosevelt Presidential Library: 70; Library of Congress: 72.

Printed in Malaysia (T)
1 3 5 6 4 2

Contents

When President George W. Bush floated plans to privatize Social Security, then-Senator Barack Obama, left, spoke out against the plan, along with senior Senator Dick Durbin (D–Illinois).

Social Security

When Social Security began in 1935, it marked the first time that the U.S. government had stepped in to create a system of retirement benefits for Americans after they had completed their working careers. Before Social Security was enacted, the older Americans who could no longer work had to rely on their children for financial aid or were forced to go to the "poorhouse." The original law covered only part of the American workforce—mainly those engaged in manufacturing and private business. Over the next two decades more and more workers, such as farmers and maintenance employees, were covered. In addition, Social Security added both disability insurance for those who could no longer work and Medicare—health care for people who were age sixty-five and older. Benefits also covered surviving spouses and children of deceased people who had been receiving Social Security benefits.

Perhaps because of its broad coverage, the Social Security system was forced to deal with serious financial problems, especially during the 1970s and 1980s. Benefits had been tied to the cost of living, which increased enormously due to high inflation. As a result, a presidential commission was formed in 1983 that helped stabilize the financing for Social Security benefits in the years ahead. Meanwhile, since 1935, the Supreme Court had been handing down a series of rulings upholding the constitutionality of the Social Security program, as well as clarifying the benefits due to widows and widowers and to the disabled. By the early twenty-first century, however, the Social Security system was facing severe financial problems. These arose as a great number of workers were due to retire. During the Republican administration of George W. Bush, the federal government debated ways of dealing with these problems, including requiring contributions by each worker into a private investment account and reducing Social Security payments by the federal government. These measures were defeated in Congress, but severe financial strains on the Social Security system continued. In addition, the rising cost of health care has added to the burdens on Social Security and Medicare, requiring creative solutions in the years ahead.

CHAPTER ONE

The Origins of Social Security

"Once I built a railroad, I made it run, made it race
  against time.
Once I built a railroad; now it's done. Brother, can
  you spare a dime?
Once I built a tower, up to the sun, brick, and rivet,
  and lime;
Once I built a tower, now it's done. Brother, can
  you spare a dime?

Say, don't you remember, they called me Al; it was
  Al all the time.
Say, don't you remember, I'm your pal? Brother,
  can you spare a dime?"

When this song, "Brother, Can You Spare a Dime?" was written in 1931 by E. Y. Harburg and Jay Gorney, the United States was in the depths of the Great Depression. About 25 percent of American workers had lost their jobs, leaving 15 million people unemployed. Peter Bernstein, a reporter for the *New York Times*, grew up in New York City

During the days of the Great Depression, millions were unemployed and homeless, without government assistance. Here, men with nowhere else to go sleep on mats in a common sleeping area in Cincinnati, Ohio.

during the Depression. "There was a time," he wrote, "when the streets of Manhattan were filled with unshaven men in threadbare clothes, their collars turned up against the cold, their shoes stuffed with newspaper to plug holes in the soles." Others were selling apples on street corners for a few pennies apiece to earn money. However, there were so many apple sellers and so few people who could afford to buy apples that no one could make much money.

The unemployed had almost nowhere to turn for help. Churches and other private organizations were providing some food for the needy. But there were millions of them and not enough to feed everyone. In New York, under Mayor Fiorello La Guardia, the city tried to provide some financial aid to the unemployed. The mayor worked closely with banks, trying to prevent them from foreclosing on the mortgages of city homeowners. Nevertheless, the city had too little money from its tax collections to help most people.

For each family that was struggling, there were also elderly relatives struggling too. Many of them lived with their children or depended on them for some financial support. Others who had retired had seen their savings wiped out in the many bank failures that occurred during the Depression. Fewer than one percent of retired workers had a pension— retirement income from their companies—in the 1930s. The rest were thrown on the mercy of charitable organizations in order to survive. Or they went to the poorhouse— homes for the needy run by local governments.

THE BEGINNINGS OF CHANGE

As the Depression grew worse, some states began to pass laws to help the unemployed and the elderly. In New York, for example, Governor Franklin Roosevelt, with the help of

Frances Perkins, one of his top aides, introduced legislation to provide unemployment insurance and old-age benefits. In 1932 Roosevelt left the governor's mansion to campaign for president of the United States. Touting a "new deal" for the American people, Roosevelt promised new measures to put Americans back to work and to replace the ineffective efforts of Republican president Herbert Hoover, who had been unable to stem the impact of the Depression. Roosevelt was elected by a huge majority.

In 1933 Roosevelt went to Washington, taking Perkins with him as his new secretary of labor. She became the first female cabinet member in the history of the United States. As the new administration took control, Congress had introduced legislation to help states provide unemployment insurance and old-age pensions. In June 1935 Roosevelt organized the Committee on Economic Security (CES) to bring all of these economic measures together and offer comprehensive legislation to the Congress. "I place the security of the men, women and children of the Nation first," Roosevelt said. Heading the CES was Labor Secretary Perkins. Meanwhile, the administration had introduced a series of new programs aimed at reviving the economy and providing jobs for the unemployed.

Roosevelt was opposed to instituting a dole—giving money away to the unemployed. Instead, he wanted the government to make money available to state and local communities so they could create jobs. The president also believed that the elderly needed an insurance program that was based on their former earnings that would help support them during retirement. As Roosevelt explained to Perkins, "I see no reason why every child, from the day he is born, shouldn't be a member of the social security system. When he begins to

Frances Perkins became the first female cabinet member in 1933 when President Franklin D. Roosevelt named her secretary of labor. It became one of the most important jobs in his administration.

grow up, he should know he will have old-age benefits direct from the insurance system to which he will belong all his life."

CRAFTING THE NEW LEGISLATION

After the CES was organized, Perkins began putting together a team to craft legislation providing a federal program for unemployment compensation and old age benefits. Heading the group on retirement benefits was Barbara Nachtrieb Armstrong, a law professor from the University of California. A brilliant, sharp-tongued woman, she had become the first female law professor in the United States. Working along with Armstrong was Murray Latimer, a quiet man— very much the opposite of his boss—who was considered the leading expert on pension programs in the United States. Princeton University professor J. Douglas Brown was also a member of the team.

As they worked together on the program, Armstrong, Latimer, and Brown were convinced that any retirement system for the elderly could not be voluntary. It should require employers and employees to contribute to the insurance plan. Otherwise some would not participate, reducing the size of the retirement-benefit pool. They also believed that the federal government, not each individual state, should run the program so it would be uniform, providing the same benefits across the United States. Making it a federal program would also reduce the complexity of the record keeping that would be required if each state kept separate records.

As the legislative team considered such a program, however, serious problems came to light. First, they were unsure whether the U.S. Constitution gave the federal government the power to establish this type of universal insurance. In 1935 the U.S. Supreme Court had ruled that a new pension program for railroad workers run by the federal government was unconstitutional. The government did not have power under the Constitution, the court said, to regulate the financial relationship between a private employer and its employees.

The Roosevelt administration hoped to get around that problem by using the taxation power of the federal government. Article 1 of the Constitution states that "The Congress shall have the Power to lay and collect Taxes . . . to . . . provide for the general Welfare of the United States." The CES team was planning to tax both employers and employees, collect their money into a large fund, and use it to provide retirement benefits.

But there was another problem. Republicans as well as some Democrats were opposed to legislation that provided unemployment benefits and old-age pensions. Many European governments had passed similar legislation decades earlier. But the tradition in the United States was a combination of rugged individualism and free enterprise. Americans were expected to take care of themselves or turn to their families or, as a last resort, ask for help from local poorhouses or charities. In addition, many congressional leaders feared that a federal insurance program would cut into the business of privately operated insurance companies. They already sold people retirement insurance—called annuities—that might no longer be purchased once a federal program was put in place.

INTRODUCING THE NEW PROGRAM

Nevertheless, Armstrong and her team completed work on their plan and, with the approval of President Roosevelt, the new legislation was introduced to Congress in 1935. Called

15

The Townsend Plan proposed that each retired person in the United States receive a government pension of $200 each month, which each person would be required to spend before he or she received the next monthly check. In 1933, that was an enormous amount of money.

the Economic Security Act of 1935, it later became known as the Social Security Act.

No sooner was the bill introduced in Congress than it came under a barrage of criticism. In 1933 Dr. Francis Townsend of Long Beach, California, had introduced a plan that would provide care for the elderly. Finding himself with no financial resources at age sixty-six, Townsend proposed that the federal government provide each retired person with $200 per month. In turn, each recipient would be required to spend this money before receiving the next monthly check, to give a boost to the failing economy. The Townsend Plan had attracted several million supporters across the country, many of whom told their congressional representatives to support the proposal. But the plan seemed far too expensive in the midst of a Depression.

The Townsend Plan was much more generous than the pension plan proposed by the Social Security Act. Armstrong's program was never designed to provide enough to cover an individual's complete financial needs during retirement. Under its provisions an individual would be eligible for no more than $85 per month, and usually far less, at age sixty-five. The amount was based on the size of his or her yearly income and the taxes paid into Social Security as well as the tax payments made by the individual's employers. But the Republicans in Congress believed that even this small amount was far too generous. Republican legislators argued that imposing additional taxes to fund Social Security would create too heavy a burden on businesses already struggling to survive during the Depression.

On the Democratic side Senator Bennett Champ Clark of Missouri argued that the proposed Social Security legislation would undermine the annuity business of many insurance companies. Instead, he proposed that any company that provided its own pension program could choose not to participate in the Social Security program. But this amendment might have destroyed the entire program, as author Nancy Altman, a recognized expert and presidential advisor on Social Security, has pointed out. "The most prosperous companies and employees would opt out [because they could afford their own programs], while the struggling companies would stay in [the much cheaper federal program], making the contribution base narrow and insecure."

Nevertheless, the Clark amendment was passed in the Senate. However, the House of Representatives adopted the Social Security Act without any such provision. Following the passage of the program in each house of Congress, members representing both houses gathered together in conference to try to iron out their differences and pass a bill. However, each side refused to budge on the Clark amendment—the Senate wanted it in the bill, while the House absolutely did not.

The conference committee decided to ask three staff members to do further research into the provisions of the Clark amendment. Their task was to find out if some form of the amendment could remain in the Social Security bill without destroying it. When the staffers reported back, after some preliminary research, that months of additional work would be necessary to craft an amendment, the House and Senate legislators decided that the needs of the elderly were too important to wait. They finally agreed to remove the amendment but to continue to research it in the future.

In August 1935 the Social Security Act became law. Title I and Title II created an insurance program for the elderly and paid benefits to the elderly poor who could not afford to pay Social Security taxes. Title III created unemployment benefits for workers who had lost their jobs. (Unemployment insurance later became a joint federal-state program that is separate from Social Security.) For the federal government it marked a new approach to safeguarding the needs of America's workers and retirees.

Andrea Gritti served as the leader of Venice from age sixty-eight to age eighty-three.

CHAPTER TWO

Attitudes Toward Aging

From the ancient world to the early twentieth century the lives of the elderly—people age sixty and older—present conflicting pictures. "I'll certainly tell you how it strikes me," said a rich, elderly manufacturer named Cephalus to the Greek philosopher Socrates in the fifth century BCE. Cephalus explained that many of his friends complained about old age and "grumble that their families show no respect for their age. . . ." Cephalus believed that his friends were "putting the blame in the wrong place" by complaining about their families. "In all this," Cephalus added, "there is only one thing to blame; and that is not their old age, Socrates, but their character. For if men are sensible and good tempered, old age is easy enough to bear: if not, youth as well as age is a burden."

Some elderly men and women, like the wealthy Cephalus, may have found old age relatively satisfying. They were admired by family and friends, probably because they were rich. In the ancient world, according to historian Tim Parkin, children were expected to care for their parents in old age. For adults this was a way of "repaying the debt" to their parents for rearing them.

The Greek philosopher Hierocles wrote, "For our parents, therefore, we should provide food freely, and such as is fitting for the weakness of old age; besides this, a bed, sleep, oil, a bath, and clothing—in short, general physical necessities, so they should never lack any of these things; thus we imitate the care they took in rearing ourselves when we were infants."

But this did not mean that children necessarily repaid that debt gladly. Parkin cited a play by the Greek writer Aristophanes in which a man turned over control of his property to his son and then was poorly treated by him—given only "gruel [mush] to lick up" for his food. While the elderly could rely to some degree on their children or their spouses to care for them, clearly the best way to deal with old age was to rely on themselves. They simply continued to work and remained active in their communities.

As the Roman philosopher Cicero wrote, "Old age will only be respected if it fights for itself, maintains its rights, avoids dependence on anyone, and asserts control over its own sphere as long as life lasts." Cicero followed his own advice, remaining active as a politician and writer until his death at the age of sixty-three in 43 BCE.

Attitudes toward the elderly were very similar during the Middle Ages and the Renaissance. Historian Shulamith Shahar, in *A History of Old Age*, pointed out that only about 8 percent of the population lived into their sixties or seventies. Wars, diseases, and poor diet claimed the lives of most people before they could ever reach old age. While there were few old people, according to Shahar, the elderly never received any special respect simply because they were old. They were expected to prove themselves. Andrea Gritti, for example, was a successful diplomat and military leader in sixteenth-century Venice. He was selected as doge— leader—of Venice when he was sixty-eight and served until he was eighty-three. Old age was considered a period when some people acquired more wisdom based on their experience. For many others, however, it was seen as a time when the mind and body lost all of their energy.

Gritti was a wealthy man who lived in a magnificent home on the Grand Canal in Venice and retired in splendor. For the elderly poor, however, life was far different. Many poor men and women had to keep working to support themselves until they died. Men worked small farms in the countryside or ran shops from their homes in towns or cities. Once they died, women who outlived their husbands might take over these shops or continue running the farms. Others moved in together to share expenses.

Most of the elderly poor wanted to remain independent. But some became physically unable to fend for themselves. Those people could try to find a place for themselves in a hospital run by one of the churches. Originally, these hospitals had been established to provide short-term lodging for travelers. Gradually, they also began to offer places for the elderly to end their lives when they could no longer maintain a household. These hospitals were also known as almshouses. During the eighteenth and nineteenth centuries they provided alms—charitable donations and services—to the elderly poor who could no longer support themselves.

Others remained at home, but they were supported by the

community. In England the Poor Law established small pensions for the elderly poor to help them support themselves. Historian David Troyansky explained, in *A History of Old Age*, that as many as one-third of the elderly in one community depended on financial aid. Troyansky wrote that the Poor Law reflected a belief that "a community was obligated to give economic aid to those who were old, poor, and unable to earn their own living."

Europeans believed that some of the elderly poor were worthy of support when they could no longer work. But others were regarded with disdain because they had refused to work throughout their lives. Those people were treated differently. Communities established workhouses for these aged poor, both men and women, who were considered lazy and shiftless. They were expected to do manual work, such as farming, to produce food for the workhouse.

While the elderly poor might spend their last days in a workhouse, the middle-class elderly generally spent their old age differently. If they owned a small estate or a successful business, they might hand over these enterprises to their children. In return, their children might give them an income to support themselves as well as a few rooms in the family home. Troyansky wrote that old age pensions began to develop during the seventeenth and eighteenth centuries for a few workers, mainly those who had worked for the government. Some men who had devoted their careers to government service received a small pension, but it was usually inadequate to support them in old age.

AMERICA AND EUROPE

In the seventeenth century European nations had also established colonies in North America. The new settlers constructed small towns in the wilderness, purchased land for farms, and built homesteads. The pioneers in New England seemed to respect the small number of people among them who reached old age during the first decades of these new settlements. Poet Anne Bradstreet described the various stages of life, adding:

> And last of all to act upon this stage
> Leaning upon his staff comes up Old Age. . . .
> His hoary hairs, and grave aspect made way
> And all gave ear to what he had to say.

The Puritans in New England believed that young people should respect their elders, whether they were parents running a household, political leaders guiding a community, or members of the clergy leading a church. The older members of the Puritan settlements were often important landowners. As historian Thomas Cole put it, they "generally lived long lives, sired large families, and garnered enough land to place their sons on plots near the parental homestead without surrendering title until death." Control over the land strengthened the position of these elderly men in Puritan society. However, adult children gradually began moving away from their parents' homes and established new settlements farther into the wilderness. As a result, the relationship between the young and the old changed.

During the eighteenth century the authority of the aged— who made up about 4 to 7 percent of the population— declined. In New England churches, for example, the best seats were no longer reserved for the elderly but went to the most well-to-do parishioners. Words such as "codger" began to enter the language to describe older people in a derogatory way. In the early nineteenth century jobs were opening up for young people that were taking them farther away from their parents. These younger workers were constructing new roads for settlers heading west, building canals to increase merchant traffic along the rivers, and working in small manufacturing firms. This enabled young people to establish their independence and undermined respect for the elderly.

As Thomas Jefferson wrote in 1815, when he was an elderly man, "Nothing is more incumbent on the old, than to know when they should get out of the way, and relinquish to younger successors the honors they can no longer earn, and the duties they can no longer perform." In 1827 clergyman Nathaniel Emmons finally retired from his church in New England at eighty-two. Out of appreciation for his long years of service, his parishioners gave him $150 annually for the rest of his life. But he was among the few retired clergy to receive such a pension. Most were expected to support themselves when they retired, and most sank into poverty, along with their wives.

Among the popular images from this era is Rip Van Winkle, a character in a story written by author Washington Irving and published in 1819. Rip fell asleep and awakened twenty years later to find that American society had changed. As an elderly man with a white beard, he felt out of place in the new world, as he was incapable of contributing to society. "Rip's fate foreshadows the obsolescence of the old man in a . . . society," wrote Cole, "where . . . productivity becomes the primary criterion of a man's worth. . . ." The same could be said for old women.

The aged in nineteenth-century America presented a conflicting portrait for the rest of society. On the one hand they

In this lithograph, Rip Van Winkle is shown suddenly waking up to a world completely different from the one he had always known.

could serve as role models of patience and peace for younger people. On the other hand highly respected preachers like Albert Barnes told his congregation in 1868 that seventy was long enough for an individual to live. "It is an advantage," he added, "to the world that men should die; that, having accomplished the great purpose of life, they should give place to others."

Self-help books on aging written in the later part of the nineteenth century urged people to safeguard their health, stay busy, and continue to play a useful role in society. The aged were warned not to become a burden to their children or to the rest of society, who might need to care for them. But this became more and more difficult as the United States became an industrialized society. The aged did not possess the physical strength to work long hours in factories, nor did many of them have the financial resources to support themselves without working.

In the early twentieth century American author E. T. Devine explained that the speed of the manufacturing process "wears out its workers with great rapidity. The young, the vigorous, the adaptable, the supple of limb, the alert of mind, are in demand. Middle age is old age."

Although many of the elderly continued to work, they were often pushed out of full-time jobs into part-time work. Some continued doing farmwork; others were employed part-time in fishing or worked as handymen and janitors. However, if an elderly person lost a job, it was almost impossible for him or her to find a new one—the person was considered too old to work.

Those who did not or who were unable to continue working at their jobs often went to live with their children. Others went to an old age home or a poor farm. A poor farm

Before the Social Security Act was passed, out-of-work seniors were relegated to poor farms or places such as these called Hoovervilles, camps for displaced persons. They were named after President Herbert Hoover, who was viewed as having done nothing to come to the aid of the poor.

had barns and animals that were tended by the elderly as well as fields in which crops were planted and harvested. There were large rooms filled with beds where the elderly poor slept. After they died, they were generally buried in unmarked graves. Some of these poor farms were not closed until the 1940s and 1950s.

During the course of a lifetime it was almost impossible for most people to save enough money to support themselves if they stopped working in old age. Retirement, as it is known today, was almost unheard of except for the very wealthy. As the chapter heading of a government report titled "The Economic Problems of Old Age" put it, "A man's productive, wage-earning period is rarely more than 45 years. Under present conditions he must earn enough in this period to contribute toward the support of aged parents, rear and educate children, maintain his family at a standard of living more or less consistent with American ideals, and save enough in the form of insurance or absolutely safe investment to provide a modest income until death, if he survives his working period. This last item of his budget is the one . . . most easily disregarded among many financial demands."

By 1935 poorhouses existed in almost every state. And most of the people living there were the aged. A study of a Massachusetts poorhouse revealed that more than 90 percent of its residents had arrived when they were older than sixty. The majority of the residents were men, because it was easier for widows to remain at home with financial aid from their children because they knew how to cook for themselves and clean their homes.

As author Nancy Altman wrote, "The poorhouse was a fate to be dreaded." Seniors often found themselves living with "whatever dregs of society happen to need the institution's shelter . . . the crude and ignorant and feeble-minded," according to a New York State report issued in 1930. And the number of poorhouse residents was increasing during the Great Depression. As the Depression began, about 50 percent of the aged population had too little money to support themselves, according to surveys in New York and Wisconsin. And this problem grew worse as the Depression continued.

CHAPTER THREE

Social Security— The Early Years

"Young people have come to wonder what would be their lot when they came to old age," said President Franklin Roosevelt when he signed the Social Security Act in 1935. "We can never insure one hundred percent of the population against one hundred percent of the hazards and vicissitudes of life, but we have tried to frame a law which will give some measure of protection to the average citizen and to his family against . . . poverty-ridden old age."

The Social Security Act provided just that—"some measure of protection." It was designed to prevent the elderly, age sixty-five and over, from living in total poverty. President Roosevelt did not believe in creating a welfare program that would support people who did not work. Instead, he wanted to create an insurance program—a reward for those who had worked all their lives—to ensure that, when they stopped bringing in an income, they were not faced with poverty. Roosevelt intended to collect money in the form of taxes from both employees

President Franklin D. Roosevelt (seated) signed the Social Security Act into law on August 14, 1935. From left are: Chairman Doughton of the House Ways and Means committee; Sen. Wagner, D-NY, coauthor of the bill; Secretary of Labor Frances Perkins; Chairman Harrison of the Senate Finance Committee; and Rep. Lewis, D-MD, another coauthor.

and employers. Each employer and employee would be taxed at one percent of an employee's income up to $3,000. (That would be the equivalent of $43,000 in present-day income.) The tax was kept low because the United States was in the midst of the Depression, wages were low, and workers could not afford to give up much money.

Approximately 26 million working people were included in the original insurance program. They represented less than half of the American workforce. They worked in manufacturing firms, like the steel industry, and businesses, such as large department stores, located across the United States. These workers had their Social Security taxes taken out of their paychecks by their employers each month. At first the Roosevelt administration wanted to provide benefits to all workers under Social Security. But there was strong opposition from powerful Republicans. They believed that it would be difficult to collect payments from farmworkers or house cleaners, whose employers—farmers and individual home owners—probably would not take out payroll taxes. The payroll taxes were slated to be instituted in 1937, with benefits starting to be paid out in 1942. These benefits averaged about $25 per month—equal to $359 in today's dollars. It was a small amount of money, but enough to allow recipients to avoid complete poverty. Since the payments were small, some congressmen who had opposed a larger Social Security program were willing to support the new program.

The Social Security Act also created a Social Security Board to run the program. The three-member board included former New Hampshire governor John Winant as chairman, Vincent Miles, a political leader from Arkansas, and Assistant Secretary of Labor Arthur Altmeyer. Altmeyer was an expert on Social Security and was considered the key member of the board.

The Social Security Board faced the enormous job of organizing the new program. This meant gathering information on more than 26 million workers, keeping track of their earnings, collecting taxes through their employers, and finally paying benefits. Thousands of new employees had to

Arthur Altmeyer,

Born in DePere, Wisconsin, in 1891, Altmeyer was raised by his grandmother after his parents divorced. He went to work for his uncle, an attorney, when he was fourteen years old, doing odd jobs in his office. With the money he earned, Altmeyer paid for his college education at the University of Wisconsin. There he studied under Professor John R. Commons, who wrote America's first worker's compensation law, providing financial payments to workers injured at their jobs. Altmeyer had read a pamphlet describing the law and later wrote, "I read it and got interested in it, and decided that I was going to [train with] Professor Commons and study labor legislation."

After graduating with honors in 1914, Altmeyer first became Commons's research assistant on legislation designed to help working people. Altmeyer later joined the Wisconsin State Industrial Commission, headed by his friend and former university classmate Edwin Witte. During the Depression Altmeyer traveled to Washington, D.C., hoping to convince the Roosevelt administration to provide funds to help the unemployed in Wisconsin. While there he worked with Labor Secretary Frances Perkins, who asked him to join the Department of Labor. As a member of the Labor Department, he commuted for a while between Washington and Wisconsin until finally deciding to return home.

No sooner had he arrived in Wisconsin, however, than he received a telegram from Labor Secretary Perkins, who appointed him assistant secretary of labor. Later in the 1930s, when he became a member of the Social Security Board, Altmeyer worked closely with the committee drafting the Social Security legislation and was named the board's chairman in 1937. He was known as Mr. Social Security

Mr. Social Security

because of his broad expertise in crafting Social Security legislation and his successful efforts to expand the program. "When the public turns to Government," Altmeyer said, "some people become frightened about dangers they think they see at the end of that road. I do not share their fear. I think that, in our democracy, Government is an instrument for the public service and an expression of the public will."

In 1946 the Social Security Board was renamed the Social Security Administration, and Altmeyer became its first commissioner. He continued to run the Social Security program until his retirement in 1953. Afterward, he remained a consultant to the Social Security Administration, helping it draft major pieces of new legislation. Altmeyer died in 1972.

This photo shows some of the 2,500 clerks working in the U.S. Census Bureau office in St. Louis, Missouri, in 1935, who were given the task of cataloging the names of those who would be considered eligible for Social Security benefits.

be hired and trained to work in Social Security offices that were established across the United States. Since America was in the midst of a depression, these government jobs were highly prized by workers who had lost their jobs.

Each worker included in the Social Security program was to be assigned a nine-digit Social Security number and given a Social Security card. Applications for numbers were delivered by postal carriers, whose job was to go house to house, delivering the mail. They helped workers fill out applications, collected them, sent them to Social Security offices, and returned with the new cards. The lowest known Social Security number, which was 001-01-0001, was assigned to Grace D. Owen of Concord, New Hampshire, who filled out her card on the first day of the application process.

THE BATTLE FOR SOCIAL SECURITY CONTINUES

The passage of the Social Security Act did not stop many Republicans from criticizing the new program. In 1936 Kansas governor Alfred Landon was the Republican nominee for president in the race against Franklin Roosevelt, who was running for a second term in the White House. Landon and other Republicans constantly pointed out during the presidential campaign that workers had to start paying Social Security taxes in 1937 but would receive no benefits until 1942. They added that many workers, such as those employed in agriculture, were not covered by the Social Security system. The Republicans also warned that the government, under the Social Security system, planned to collect money from America's workers and put it in a large reserve fund to pay people once they retired. In the meantime, according to the Republicans, the Roosevelt administration planned to spend this money on other projects. Such a large reserve fund was not necessary, they argued. Instead, the government could collect far less money in payroll taxes to fund Social Security benefits.

As part of their campaign literature the Republicans sent

out a pamphlet to millions of workers proclaiming: *"You're sentenced* TO A WEEKLY PAY REDUCTION for ALL OF YOUR WORKING LIFE. YOU'LL HAVE TO *SERVE THE SENTENCE* UNLESS YOU HELP TO REVERSE IT NOV. 3, ELECTION DAY." Landon lost the election in a landslide, but this did not end the controversy over Social Security.

The original law had called for a large cash reserve, funded by Social Security taxes, to be set up and invested in government bonds. Republicans led by Senator Arthur Vandenberg continued to argue that such a large reserve was unnecessary. Instead, payroll taxes could be reduced and a much smaller reserve created.

Vandenberg said that this would put Social Security much closer to a pay-as-you go basis. Since the number of retirees would be quite small during the early years of the program and the number of workers paying into the program quite large, a big reserve was unnecessary. This was known as the dependency ratio—the number of retirees collecting benefits compared to the number of workers supporting them. In addition, the replacement ratio was also quite favorable. This was the size of the retirement benefit—which was quite small—compared to the average earnings of employees— which was much higher.

In 1937 the Social Security Board established an advisory council to consider Social Security financing as well as other issues. The twenty-five-member council included people from business as well as labor unions who represented millions of American workers. As the council was being established, the Supreme Court handed down a ruling in a legal case relating to Social Security. In its decision of mid–May 1937 in *Steward Machine Co.* v. *Collector of Internal Revenue*, the majority of the Court agreed that Congress was authorized to pass the new program under the Constitution because it promoted the general welfare of the American people.

With support from the Supreme Court decision, the advisory council continued meeting and issued a final report late in 1938. The report backed a financing plan that was more pay-as-you-go, but with a trust fund holding some cash reserves in case of emergencies. Benefits were to start being paid in 1940 rather than 1942. Since 1940 was an election year, this would please a number of older workers who were approaching retirement and who were thought to be more likely to reelect their congressmen if the benefits were paid.

In addition, the formula for calculating benefits was changed. The original law had called for the size of the retirement benefit to be based on the total amount of wages a worker had earned during his or her years on the job. But this meant that anyone who had become sick or disabled and could no longer work would be penalized with a lower benefit. The new formula calculated benefits on the basis of the average amount of wages earned during a worker's years of employment. This did not penalize a worker who dropped out of the workforce for a period of time because of illness and then returned, or someone who had become disabled and could no longer work. Thus, the years that someone did not work were not used in calculating his or her Social Security benefits.

The council also recommended that Social Security benefits be expanded to cover the families of retired workers. At age sixty-five, spouses of retired workers would qualify for benefits that were half the amount received by the workers. If a worker entitled to Social Security died, his widow and their young, dependent children, up to age eighteen, would be entitled to a benefit of 50 percent of the amount that would have been received by the retired worker.

These measures prevented the families of retired workers from sinking into poverty after the worker's death. It also increased the benefits for a retired worker and spouse. For example, the worker who received a monthly benefit of $34.83 saw it increase to $52.25 to include his spouse.

The council's recommendations were approved by President Roosevelt and sent to Congress. Legislators added an amendment called the Federal Insurance Contributions Act (FICA), specifying how payroll taxes would be collected. In fact, payroll taxes are now often referred to as FICA. The council's recommendations and the amendment were overwhelmingly passed by Congress in 1939. A year later Ida May Fuller of Vermont became the first person to receive a Social Security check—one of 222,000 people, adults as well as children, who began to receive benefits. Her monthly check was $22.54. Average monthly earnings in 1940 were about $100.

MORE CHANGES FOR SOCIAL SECURITY

On December 7, 1941, the Japanese attacked the U.S. fleet anchored in Pearl Harbor, Hawaii. As a result, the United States entered World War II, which had begun two years earlier. U.S. forces joined Great Britain and France in fighting against the Axis powers—Nazi Germany, Italy, and Japan. The war effort required American industry to vastly increase production. Many older workers postponed retirement to remain in the workforce at factories that were producing tanks, planes, guns, and other war supplies. In addition, hundreds of thousands of young men in the workforce joined the armed forces to fight in the war. Their places on factory assembly

Ida M. Fuller, seventy-six, of Ludlow, Vermont, holds up her Social Security check for $41.30 in this October 4, 1950, photo, after Congress voted for an 80 percent raise in benefits.

lines were often taken by women. With more people working and others postponing retirement, contributions to the Social Security Trust Funds increased enormously. In addition, the number of retirees drawing benefits was lower than expected because so many people postponed retirement—keeping the dependency ratio favorable. Finally, benefits remained low while wages increased during the war years, keeping the replacement ratio very favorable, too.

President Roosevelt died in 1945, shortly before the war ended in Europe. He was succeeded by his vice president, Harry Truman. Truman wanted to expand Social Security to include many of the people who had not been covered under the original legislation. They included farmworkers, janitors and house cleaners, schoolteachers, and hospital employees. These jobs were overwhelmingly held by women. The number of African Americans and other minorities covered by the program remained extremely low.

Social Security Commissioner Arthur Altmeyer agreed that changes to the program were necessary, and he proposed establishing another advisory council, which was approved by Congress. The new council was headed by Robert Ball, who had joined the Social Security Administration in 1939. He had just married and needed a job. One of his professors in college had told him, "This program is just starting up. It's going to be a big program. It's an attractive program and an important social program, and it would be a good thing if you got in on it in the beginning." He began working in the Newark, New Jersey, Social Security office and later transferred to Baltimore, Maryland. His work examining possible improvements to the Social Security program had impressed J. Douglas Brown, a member of the advisory council and one of the architects of the original Social Security law, as well as several other council members. They proposed that he lead the new working group.

The council recommended increasing benefits and offering them to farmworkers, household workers, and self-employed people who had not been covered by the original legislation. The recommendation was sent to Congress, which debated the bill in its 1949–1950 session, before it was passed overwhelmingly by the Senate and the House of Representatives. The 1950 law included an 80-percent increase in benefits, from an average of $25 monthly to $46 monthly. (Average monthly earnings were $240.) The new law also extended coverage to 10 million additional uninsured workers.

The 1950 legislation signified a great improvement in Social Security because it covered so many more workers. Congress considered adding health insurance and disability payments for elderly workers to the bill, but these proposals were defeated. They were considered too expensive by many members of Congress, and powerful lobbying groups such as the American Medical Association opposed them. However, these changes would be made in the decades ahead.

President Dwight D. Eisenhower was responsible for extending Social Security benefits to 10 million previously excluded worker categories.

CHAPTER FOUR

Social Security— 1950s–1990s

"Government is an instrument for the public service and an expression of the public will," wrote Arthur Altmeyer. "We strengthen our democracy, and our faith in the processes of our democracy, when we make it possible for our Government to serve us by doing for us what we want but cannot do for ourselves acting as individuals." In 1953 Altmeyer retired as commissioner of the Social Security Administration. But the new president, Republican Dwight Eisenhower, continued the work Altmeyer had begun.

In 1954 the Eisenhower administration proposed to Congress that Social Security coverage be made available to 10 million workers who had not been included in previous amendments. Among them were farm owners, farmworkers not covered by the 1950 amendment, and those who were self-employed. The new bill also took up the disability issue.

Disabled workers who had been unable to contribute to

Social Security after they could no longer work were penalized with low retirement benefits because Social Security benefits were based on average wages. To calculate the benefits of the disabled, their wages before the disability were averaged in with the zero wages they had earned when they could no longer work. To deal with this problem, the new legislation established a disability freeze. Social Security benefits were to be figured only on the average wage before the disability. Finally, the new bill called for regular advisory councils similar to the council that had served during the 1930s to be appointed by the federal government. These amendments were passed by huge margins in both the House of Representatives and the Senate in 1954.

That year the House and Senate, which were both controlled by Democrats, took up the issue of making disability insurance a part of Social Security for all those who could no longer work. The House Committee on Ways and Means, which considered all monetary bills in the House of Representatives before they reached the entire House, proposed limiting insurance to workers between fifty and sixty-four who had become disabled. This would be far less costly than a bill covering younger disabled workers. This bill was overwhelmingly passed by the House, 356 to 8, before being considered by the Senate. The Eisenhower administration and most Republicans in the Senate were opposed to creating disability insurance and did not want it to become part of Social Security. Nevertheless, Democrats in the Senate, like the majority of members in the House, added an amendment to include disability insurance as part of Social Security. The vote in the Senate on the amendment was very close. There, the bill passed 47 to 45 in 1956 and became law after it was signed by President Eisenhower.

Wilbur Cohen

One of the people most instrumental in the passage of Medicare was the assistant secretary of health, education, and welfare, Wilbur Cohen. Born in Milwaukee, Wisconsin, in 1913, Cohen graduated from the University of Wisconsin in 1934. Afterward, he went to Washington, D.C., where he worked as a researcher for the committee that designed the Social Security legislation of 1935. Cohen was a friend and trusted assistant of Edwin Witte and Arthur Altmeyer, both of whom helped shape the Social Security programs. He later worked in the Social Security Administration and was appointed assistant secretary of health, education, and welfare in 1961.

Cohen had suggested the disability plan that became part of the Social Security legislation in the 1950s and was a strong advocate of the disability insurance that was finally enacted into law during the 1950s and 1960s. He had also spent many years trying to interest congressional legislators in a health-care program for the elderly. Indeed, as one of the principal architects of the Medicare legislation passed in 1965, he became known among Washington political leaders as "The Man Who Built Medicare." Appointed secretary of health, education, and welfare in 1968 by President Johnson, Cohen later left government service and became a professor of public welfare administration at the University of Michigan. He died in 1987.

Disability insurance had been strongly opposed by the American Medical Association, which believed that the government was gradually taking over more and more control of the practice of medicine. For many years the AMA had also opposed a government-run program of health insurance for the elderly. Lawmakers favored it, as did the powerful labor unions. In 1960 Democrats—led by Ways and Means Chairman Wilbur Mills and Senator Robert Kerr of Oklahoma—worked out a compromise. Large medical bills for illnesses such as cancer or heart disease could easily impoverish a retired couple, forcing them to sell their home and spend all of their savings. The Kerr-Mills Bill, which became law in 1960, provided money to pay the medical bills of elderly people who might have otherwise become impoverished if they had been forced to pay these bills themselves. Congress also extended disability insurance coverage to workers younger than age fifty. Workers were covered for physical and mental illness as well as disability due to blindness.

SOCIAL SECURITY CHANGES IN THE 1960S

The new law marked a big step in expanding disability coverage under Social Security. But Democratic president John F. Kennedy, elected in 1960, intended to go a giant step further. In a speech to a crowd of about 20,000 people at Madison Square Garden in New York in 1962, Kennedy described the economic conditions facing retirees if they became sick. The husband, Kennedy said, "might have been a clerk or a salesman . . . or worked in a factory." He owned a house, had a retirement pension, had about twenty-five-hundred dollars in the bank, and began collecting Social Security. "And then his wife gets sick. . . . First goes the twenty-five hundred dollars. . . . Next he mortgages his house. . . . Then he goes to

President Lyndon B. Johnson signs the Medicare bill into law as (left to right) Lady Bird Johnson, Vice President Hubert H. Humphrey, Bess Truman, and former president Harry S. Truman look on.

49

his children, who themselves are heavily burdened. . . . Then their savings begin to go."

President Kennedy was assassinated before he could lead the effort to create a retiree health-care program. But his successor, Lyndon Johnson, took up where Kennedy had left off. Johnson proposed a series of programs, called the Great Society, which were designed to improve the lives of the poor and the elderly. Among them was a health plan called Medicare. Part A of Medicare, which was mandatory and financed as Social Security is—from employer and employee payroll taxes—paid for hospital costs. Part B, which was voluntary and financed by payments from participants, covered the cost of physicians. A separate program, called Medicaid, was funded by both the federal government and the states, but each state administered its own program. It was designed to pay the medical costs of the poor and the low-income elderly.

In 1965, the year after Johnson's election, Medicare and Medicaid were approved by Congress. "No longer will older Americans be denied the healing miracle of modern medicine," Johnson said. "No longer will illness crush and destroy the savings that they have so carefully put away over a lifetime so that they might enjoy the dignity in their later years."

While Social Security was expanding its programs, Congress was also increasing monthly benefits during the 1960s to keep up with inflation—the rise in the cost of living. Meanwhile, payroll taxes had increased from 4.4 percent in 1967 to 4.8 percent in 1969, and the amount of earnings taxed had risen to $7,800 in 1968. (The average yearly earning for a manufacturing worker was between $6,000 and $7,000.)

In 1972 Congress established the Supplemental Security Income program (SSI). SSI provides income for the elderly poor, as well as the poor who are blind or disabled. Although

SSI is administered by the Social Security Administration, it is completely separate from Social Security. SSI is a federal-state welfare program designed to give those who need it a minimum income.

At the same time, new legislation was passed by Congress to index Social Security benefits. Benefits were correlated to rising wages as well as the rising cost of living. This meant that yearly benefits would increase automatically when the cost of living—the price of food, housing, clothing, etc.—increased by 3 percent or more annually. Called a cost of living adjustment (COLA), it enabled benefits to keep pace with inflation. In the past, retirees had to wait for Congress to pass legislation approving a new increase, which often occurred long after the cost of living had already gone up.

Indexing assumed that inflation would remain low, as it had in the past. But during the mid-1970s inflation increased enormously. One reason was a great increase in the cost of oil. While inflation—the rise in the cost of food, housing, heat, and other essential services—between 1972 and 1976 had been predicted at 14.53 percent, in fact it was far higher, at 40.6 percent. Meanwhile, wages remained unchanged. This sent Social Security benefits soaring, and the replacement ratio—the ratio of benefits paid out to wages earned—became very unstable. At the same time, unemployment had risen to 6.5 percent, which meant that many workers had lost their jobs and were no longer paying payroll taxes to fund Social Security.

As a result, by the mid-1970s the Social Security system was running a deficit. Money being paid out in benefits was exceeding the money flowing in from payroll taxes. That deficit hit $5.6 billion in 1977, and the government had to dip into the Social Security Trust Funds to make up the difference. A report issued that year predicted that the situation would grow much worse in the years ahead. Finally, in 1977, President Jimmy Carter signed a new law adjusting the indexing formula to reduce the benefits being paid out. In addition, payroll taxes were increased, especially for higher-income workers, and the amount of earnings that could be taxed was also increased.

Nevertheless, the high rate of inflation continued. Although economists had predicted the rate at about 28 percent from 1977 to 1981, the actual rate of inflation was 60 percent. Unemployment also grew to more than 7 percent. When the Republican administration of President Ronald Reagan took office in 1981, the Social Security system was facing a severe financial crisis.

DEALING WITH THE FINANCIAL CRISIS

During his election campaign Ronald Reagan had promised to cut the size and cost of the federal government. Among the early proposals made by David Stockman, the director of the Office of Management and Budget (OMB), was a cut in Social Security benefits amounting to $2.5 billion. This cut would also help deal with the deficits that were affecting the Social Security system. Among those hardest hit would be people who had taken early retirement, at age sixty-two. Early retirees received only 8 percent of the benefit given to workers who retired at age sixty-five. Stockman proposed that their benefit be reduced from 8 percent to 5.5 percent.

The proposed changes created an uproar in Congress. Social Security was not only an extremely popular program, congressional representatives depended on votes from the elderly to win elections. Nevertheless, President Reagan believed that the "Social Security System is teetering on the

President Ronald Reagan rode into office on a promise to slash government spending, including Social Security benefits. Here he is presented with a meat cleaver by Secretary of the Interior James Watt (second from left) to assist him in trimming the budget. Also present were Treasury Secretary Donald Regan (left) and budget director David Stockman.

edge of bankruptcy," and that drastic measures were necessary. He called for a "bipartisan effort [involving both political parties] to save Social Security."

Democrats in Congress struck back, accusing the administration of "terrifying older people" to win approval of budget cuts. As author Nancy Altman explained, the federal government could have issued treasury bonds and sold them to the American public or financial institutions to raise money. There was no threat of bankruptcy.

A deadlock occurred between Congress and the Reagan administration over future financing for Social Security. As a result, in 1983 President Reagan appointed a bipartisan commission to deal with the financing issue. The fifteen-member commission was headed by economist Alan Greenspan and included members of Congress as well as business and labor leaders. One of the members chosen by Congress was Robert Ball, an expert on Social Security who had run the administration from 1962 to 1973.

The Greenspan Commission met monthly and considered a variety of alternatives. Republicans on the commission were pushing for benefit cuts. However, Ball and the Democratic members explained that this was unacceptable to them. That said, Ball recognized that something had to be done. The financial problems were expected to continue during the 1980s. Ball knew that by the 1990s, however, the dependency ratio—of workers to retirees—would be very favorable. People born during the Great Depression—a time of low birth rates—would be retiring, and there would be enough employees in the workforce to support them. This was the baby boom generation, people born between 1946 and 1964.

But by 2011 the baby boom generation would be retiring. This was an enormous group of people who would reduce the dependency ratio to about two workers for every retiree. Therefore, Ball realized that for Social Security to remain in good financial shape for the twenty-first century, changes had to be made.

As the Greenspan Commission continued meeting, the immediate financial crisis grew worse, and the Social Security Trust Funds were running out of money. Meanwhile, Ball offered suggestions that might help with the problem. Finally, he helped the members of the commission to reach a compromise. This included imposing a tax on up to half of the Social Security benefits received by retirees with an annual income of more than $20,000. In addition, the retirement age was to be raised gradually to sixty-seven, saving the Social Security system a great amount of money, because workers retiring later would wait an extra two years to receive benefits. Additional workers—those in nonprofit organizations and those newly hired by the federal government—were to be covered under Social Security and had to pay a payroll tax that increased the Social Security reserve funds. The new proposals were approved by Congress in 1983.

This legislation stabilized the Social Security system, and over the next decade it produced a surplus of money. Meanwhile, the federal budget was running up enormous deficits, and money from the Social Security Trust Funds was being used to deal with them. Some political leaders, including Senator Daniel Moynihan of New York, wanted Social Security to return to a pay-as-you-go plan to force the federal government to balance its budget. He also proposed that employees be permitted to take some of the money held back in payroll taxes and invest it themselves in the stock market as part of their individual retirement accounts. Traditionally, the stock market had performed far better and therefore made more money for investors than the treasury bonds in which Social Security invested its trust fund money.

In 1994 Social Security taxes were increased on retirees when half of their Social Security benefits, plus other income from such things as part-time work, exceeded $34,000. This change would allow more money to remain in the Social Security Trust Funds. Meanwhile, between 1994 and 1996, the Advisory Council on Social Security was meeting to consider changes in Social Security. The council realized that while the Social Security system would run a surplus until 2020, after that time the money in the trust funds would begin to decline, and full benefits would not be able to be paid to retirees by 2030. However, the members of the council disagreed over the steps that should be taken to deal with the problem. Some advocated increasing payroll taxes on Social Security benefits and investing a small part of the trust funds in the stock market. This could provide a higher return on the investment than the treasury bonds that the funds currently held. Others wanted to give workers the ability to establish individual retirement accounts with money raised from an increase in payroll taxes. Then they would be allowed to invest some of the money in stocks. In addition, the council considered paying out a flat retirement benefit instead of one based on average earnings. However, none of these proposals became part of the Social Security program.

CHAPTER FIVE

The Current Social Security System at Work

On September 11, 2001, Al-Qaeda terrorists seized control of four large passenger jet airliners. They flew two of the airplanes into the Twin Towers of the World Trade Center in New York City, a third into the Pentagon building—the headquarters of the U.S. Defense Department—just outside Washington, D.C., and the fourth into the middle of Pennsylvania. Almost three thousand people lost their lives, and families grieved for the loss of parents and children who had been killed in the tragedy.

Two days after the attack the Social Security Administration was working to identify those who had died in the terrorist attacks, as well as their families. Many of the families with loved ones who had died on 9/11 were entitled to survivor benefits. Their deceased family members had paid employment taxes into the Social Security system. While Social Security is known primarily as a source of retiree benefits, it also includes a wide range of other programs.

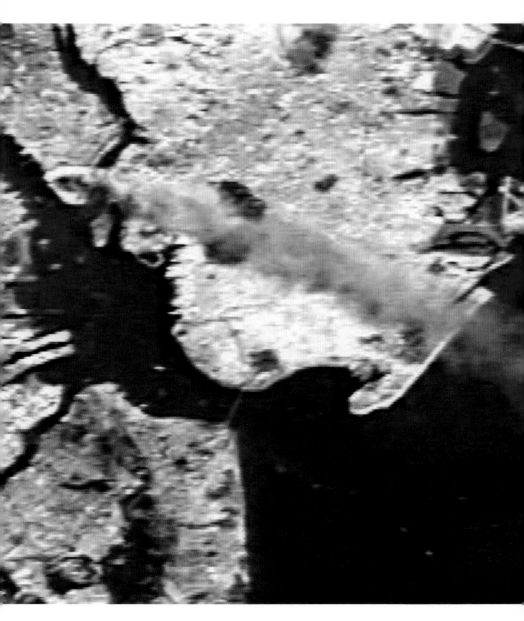

This image sent from the International Space Station shows a smoke plume rising above Manhattan on September 11, 2001, after two airplanes hit the Twin Towers of New York's World Trade Center.

Old-Age, Survivors, and Disability Insurance (OASDI) is the formal name for the programs popularly known as Social Security. Approximately 62 million people receive monthly benefits under OASDI programs. These programs were estimated to cost more than $649 billion in 2009, with an average monthly check of around $940. These checks were issued to elderly retired individuals; survivors of the elderly who have died as well as survivors of much younger workers, such as the victims of the 9/11 attacks; the elderly poor and the blind; disabled people; and those who are receiving health benefits under Medicare and Medicaid.

American citizens and noncitizens who have permission to work in the United States must have a Social Security number to get a job and eventually collect benefits. Parents can apply for a Social Security number when their child is born. A child's birth certificate is proof of his or her citizenship, which is necessary to obtain a Social Security card with a Social Security number on it. Noncitizens must produce their immigration documents at a local Social Security office to receive a number.

Each month employees and employers pay FICA taxes. The employee's share is 6.2 percent of his or her salary, and the employer pays a matching amount for each worker. This tax is paid on the first $102,000 of a worker's pay. An additional 2.9 percent is split by the employee and the employer to pay for Medicare. To qualify for Social Security benefits, a worker must earn credits on the job. In 2008, for example, employees earned one credit for each $1,050 in salary they earned at their jobs. An employee can receive up to four credits by earning $4,200 in salary annually at any time throughout the year. Workers usually qualify for benefits by earning forty credits over their working careers. That is, they can usually qualify for Social Security after ten years at work. This entitles them to receive Social Security income at retirement. A worker can choose to retire at age sixty-two or to wait until sixty-six to retire—sixty-seven for workers born in 1960 or later—which is considered the normal retirement age. Some workers, however, choose to stay at their jobs until they are age seventy, when they begin collecting Social Security. If they continue working after seventy, they do not receive greater Social Security payments.

RETIREMENT BENEFITS

Social Security uses a formula to compute a worker's Primary Insurance Amount (PIA) when he or she retires. The PIA is based on his or her average indexed monthly earnings (AIME). The benefit amount, PIA, of a person about to retire is based on an average of the worker's highest-earning thirty-five years of employment. The wages are indexed for inflation. This means that $2,000 earned in 1965 might be worth eight times more, or $16,000, forty years later, at retirement in 2005. The indexed amounts are averaged together at retirement to determine a worker's AIME. Those earning low salaries—about $20,000 per year, on average—who retire at sixty-six receive benefits equal to about 50 percent of their earnings. Those whose salaries were in the middle range—about $30,000—receive 40 percent of their salaries in Social Security benefits. And those at a higher average salary, $100,000 or more, for example, receive benefits that equal about 20 percent of their salaries. Nevertheless, the high-wage earners still receive larger Social Security checks than those who averaged smaller salaries during their working careers.

In addition, retirees receive an increase in their monthly

paycheck when the cost of living increases. In 2009, for example, the increase in the retiree benefit rose by 6 percent to match the increase in the cost of living. As a result, each retiree averaged an extra $63 per month, the greatest increase in twenty-five years.

Average earnings combined with retirement age are used to determine the size of monthly benefits. A worker who retires at sixty-two receives a lesser monthly amount than one who retires at sixty-six or seventy. For example, a man who averaged $72,000 in yearly earnings was entitled to $1,580 per month if he retired at age sixty-two, $2,031 per month if he retired at age sixty-six, and $2,713 per month if he retired at age seventy. Those who retire at sixty-two and continue working must give up $1 in Social Security benefits for every $2 they earn over an annual limit of about $13,000. Therefore, if an individual earned $20,000 ($7,000 more than $13,000), he or she would lose $3,500 ($1 for each $2 earned) in Social Security benefits. At age sixty-six, however, a retiree can collect full benefits and continue earning any amount of money.

Social Security benefits may also be taxed if an individual's total income, including paid work and investments, is greater than $25,000. For example, if a retired worker earned between $25,000 and $34,000, he or she would be required to pay a tax of up to 50 percent on the Social Security benefits received. When a person earns more than $34,000, the tax jumps to an amount up to 85 percent of Social Security benefits received.

Most retired workers have annual incomes far lower than $34,000. According the American Association of Actuaries, "Monthly benefits from Social Security represent half or more of total retirement income for about two-thirds of all Social

Security recipients aged 65 or older, and for three-quarters of those aged 75 or older. For more than one-third of Social Security recipients aged 65 or older, and 40 percent of those aged 75 or older, Social Security monthly benefits represent more than 90 percent of their total income."

Although Social Security was never designed to be the primary source of income for retirees, it has become just that for millions of retired Americans. In the past many retirees received pensions from their companies, guaranteeing them a certain amount of money each month based on their salary and years of service. But these pensions have largely disappeared because most companies can no longer afford them. Approximately 10 percent of the elderly population now lives in poverty, which is defined as an annual income of $13,000 to $14,570 for a married couple or about $10,830 to $12,460 for a single person, depending on the state in which the person lives.

As a result, some retired elderly as well as blind and disabled people are entitled to Supplemental Security Income (SSI). This program is run by federal and state governments and administered by the Social Security Administration. According to rules set by the federal government, to qualify for SSI, a person can earn a maximum of $500 to $700 per month in income for a single individual. In addition, an individual's assets—what he or she owns—must be worth less than $2,000, or $3,000 for a couple. However, items such as the individual's home or car are not included in this amount. In addition to SSI, an individual or couple may also receive Social Security, but these benefits are considered part of their income.

SOCIAL SECURITY DEPENDENTS AND SURVIVORS' BENEFITS

Not only do retirees receive Social Security payments after leaving their jobs, their dependents are also entitled to benefits from the federal government. These survivor benefits are paid to the retiree's spouse—male or female—aged sixty-two or older as well as to a younger spouse—male or female—who is caring for the dead retiree's child who is under age sixteen. The amount of the spouse's monthly check is 50 percent of what the living worker would have received each month. If a man received $900, for example, his widow is entitled to an additional $450 monthly.

Since women, on average, live longer than men—their average life expectancy is roughly eighty as compared to roughly seventy-five—survivor benefits are especially helpful to them. Poverty is a serious problem among elderly women. In 2004 the poverty rate among women older than sixty-five was 12 percent—almost twice the rate of elderly men. This is in part because women have traditionally earned less than men while working and thus collect less in Social Security benefits. They also live longer than men, using up retirement savings and other sources of income.

Survivors' benefits are also paid to a younger spouse who is caring for a dead retiree's children if those children are under age sixteen. Unmarried children under age eighteen also receive benefits. A widow, for example, receives a monthly benefit that is half the retiree's check. The surviving spouse of a worker whose average income was between $20,000 and $30,000 would receive between $800 and $1,400 each month. The monthly check for the spouse and child would be between $1,500 and $2,000, based on the deceased worker's income.

These benefits are received by spouses of survivors of the 9/11 tragedy. The amount received depends on whether the worker earned enough work credits before death to qualify for Social Security. Generally, Social Security benefits are paid when a worker has earned forty credits on the job. But the Social Security law allows younger workers to earn fewer than forty credits and still qualify for benefits. For example, a thirty-four-year-old worker need have earned only twelve work credits to have qualified for Social Security benefits at his or her death. A forty-four-year-old worker need have earned only twenty credits.

The surviving spouse receives part of what the worker's benefits would have been; a child under age sixteen also receives an additional 75 percent of the worker's benefit. For example, the spouse and child of a worker who earned $40,000 a year or more would be entitled to $1,600 to $2,400 per month in Social Security benefits. The families of lower-income workers receive less, between $800 and $1,400 per month.

DISABILITY BENEFITS

Each month Social Security benefits are paid to more than 7 million disabled people and their families. Workers qualify for disability payments, called Social Security Disability Insurance (SSDI), by earning work credits, just as they do for retirement benefits. Some of these work credits must be earned during the decade before the disability occurred. Younger workers, those aged thirty-one and younger, are required to earn fewer work credits to be eligible for SSDI, as they had less time to build up credits before the disability occurred.

The Social Security Administration defines a physical or

psychological disability as one that "is expected to last, or has lasted, at least one year . . . and prevents you from doing any substantial or gainful work." These include disabilities such as a serious heart condition, mental illness, brain damage, or incurable cancer. The disability must be verified by a physician. The Social Security Administration defines "substantial or gainful work" as the employee's current job or any other employment that a worker might be qualified to do to earn $860 or more per month.

Individuals who receive disability benefits can decide to return to work during a trial period without giving up their benefits. The trial period can be attempted every five years and lasts up to nine months. If the trial works out, the employee on disability can give up his or her benefits and return to a job. If the trial is unsuccessful, the employee can give up work and continue receiving disability payments.

HEALTH BENEFITS UNDER SOCIAL SECURITY

When Medicare became law in 1965, it was strongly opposed by powerful medical groups, such as the American Medical Association (AMA), as well as insurance companies. The AMA claimed that the federal government was taking control of health care and would dictate to doctors how they could practice medicine. While this did not happen, Medicare did set limits on what hospitals and doctors could charge their patients aged sixty-five and older.

Approximately 44 million people are covered under Medicare. The program is directed by the Social Security Administration and the federal Department of Health and Human Services. Large insurance companies contract with the government to run the program in each state. Part A of Medicare pays hospital as well as home health-care costs. It is a mandatory program, and workers pay a small percentage of their income in payroll taxes to help finance it. Those eligible for Part A include retirees and their families or their survivors. In addition, workers qualifying for disability insurance can also participate in the Medicare program.

Medicare Part A does not pay all hospital bills. There is a deductible—an amount that the patient must pay, more than $1,000 annually, before Medicare starts covering hospital costs. In addition, patients who are in a hospital more than sixty days must pay part of the cost for each day they remain. This is called a coinsurance amount, which was $267 in 2008 and doubles after ninety days. Therefore Medicare pays only part of medical costs. The patient must also pay a coinsurance amount, which is separate from the deductible.

Medicare Part B is a voluntary program for people sixty-five and older that requires them to pay a monthly fee that was about $96 in 2008. Part B covers physicians' bills as well as other costs, such as ambulances, laboratory tests, x-rays, and drugs administered in a hospital or doctor's office. Medicare Part B pays only 80 percent of the charges approved by the Medicare program. The patient must pay the rest as coinsurance, which can be a great amount of money for patients with illnesses that confine them to a hospital or a nursing home. As a result, many retirees purchase additional insurance from a private insurance company to cover the gap between what Medicare pays and the charges that still remain. This Medicare supplement is often called "medigap" insurance, and it is available from many health insurance companies.

Medigap plans cover coinsurance for Part A and an additional year in the hospital, as well as Medicare Part B coinsurance. However, some of these plans have high deductibles, as

Raymond Philpot is one of many seniors who protested President George W. Bush's plan to make changes in the Social Security and Medicare system that would put the burden on the elderly rather than the government.

much as $1,900 in 2008, that must be paid before the plan pays any expenses.

Medicare Part C provides people over sixty-five with an alternative to Part A and Part B. Medicare Part C plans are run by private insurers that are approved by the federal government. The Part C plans are often less expensive than Part A and Part B. They may also provide wider coverage, such as the cost of eyeglasses, than Part A or Part B. The disadvantage is that patients have a more limited choice of doctors and caregivers. The Part C plan specifies a list—or network—of doctors that patients must use. Part A and Part B leave the choice up to the patient.

In addition to Medicare Part A, Part B, and Part C, Congress also approved Medicare Part D, which covers prescription drugs. Beginning in 2006 retirees began paying about $32 per month to their health insurance companies to belong to the plan. Medicare Part D had a deductible of $275 per year in 2008, as well as copayments. That meant that retirees had to make up the difference—out-of-pocket expenses—from their own income. Those who could not afford the out-of-pocket expenses were given financial help from the Medicare program. To qualify, an individual had to be earning $15,600 or less.

While some retirees saved money under Medicare Part D, others found that they spent more on drugs than ever before. This is one of several controversies that have surrounded Social Security since it began. Those controversies have involved major decisions by the U.S. Supreme Court, proposals to change Social Security, and providing financing the program in the years ahead.

CHAPTER SIX

Social Security and the Supreme Court

When the Social Security Act was passed in 1935, New Dealers were concerned that the program might never be given a chance to succeed before the U.S. Supreme Court struck it down. The majority of justices on the nine-person court held very conservative views regarding the power of the federal government to influence the American economy. The justices wanted these powers severely limited to remain within what they thought was the meaning of the words written in the U.S. Constitution. New Dealers were afraid that the court's conservative majority would find the Social Security law—requiring employers and employees to pay a tax to support retirement pensions and unemployment—an unconstitutional interference with a free economy.

The court had already applied its conservative principles in several different cases. In 1918 the U.S. Congress had passed a minimum wage law for women working in the District of Columbia. The District of Columbia does not have a state

When President Franklin D. Roosevelt took office, many of the justices held conservative views. President Roosevelt came up with a way to circumvent their power that went down to a rousing defeat.

government but is administered by Congress. Under the new law the District of Columbia Minimum Wage Board, headed by Jesse Adkins, voted to raise the pay of women working in hotels and hospitals to $16.50 per week. For Willie Lyons, a twenty-one-year-old elevator operator at the Congress Hall Hotel, this meant a huge increase over what she had been receiving—$35 per month. But the hotel was unable to pay Lyons this much, and she was afraid of being fired. Lyons did not believe she could find another job that paid as well for such easy work. As a result, her lawyers asked the local court to stop the wage increase from taking effect.

At the same time a similar situation was occurring at the Children's Hospital of the District of Columbia. The hospital's lawyers also tried to persuade the local court to stop the Minimum Wage Board from enforcing the wage increase.

Although the local court upheld the right of the Minimum Wage Board to establish the new pay rates for women, the cases were appealed and eventually reached the Supreme Court. There, in the cases of *Adkins* v. *Children's Hospital* and *Adkins* v. *Lyons*, the majority of the justices ruled that the minimum-wage law was unconstitutional. The majority opinion was written by Justice George Sutherland. He stated that the law violated an individual's "liberty of contract" according to the due process clause of the Fifth Amendment. This clause states that "No person shall be . . . deprived of life, liberty, or property, without due process of law." The majority of justices reasoned that women workers were perfectly capable of negotiating their own salaries with employers, and that Congress did not have the right to interfere with their liberty to do so. And yet, at some point, a minimum wage law was passed.

In 1935 a similar case involving due process came before the Supreme Court. A year earlier Congress passed the Railroad Retirement Act. This required the nation's railroads and their employees to set aside a percentage of their incomes to fund a retirement and pension system. Congress had acted because the Constitution had given it the right to regulate interstate commerce, such as the operation

The Railroad Retirement Board turned out to be short-lived.

of railroads that ran through various states. However, the Supreme Court, in the case of *Railroad Retirement Board* v. *Alton Railroad Company*, ruled that the Retirement Act violated the due process clause.

In the early 1930s the majority of the Supreme Court justices were conservative. Popularly called the Four Horsemen of Reaction by New Dealers, who were liberal, they were justices Willis Van Devanter, James C. McReynolds, George

Sutherland, and Pierce Butler. Another group of justices took a more flexible view of the Constitution, giving the federal government more power to deal with economic emergencies than the conservatives. These liberal justices were Louis D. Brandeis, Benjamin Cardozo, and Harlan Fiske Stone. In the middle were two other justices, who did not vote consistently with either the conservatives or the liberals. These were Chief Justice Charles Evans Hughes and Justice Owen Roberts. They were known as the swing votes.

The Railroad Retirement case resulted in a close 5 to 4 decision. The majority ruled that "a railroad's assets, though dedicated to public use, remain the private property of its owners, and cannot be taken without just compensation" and therefore "violate the due process clause" of the Constitution. The majority of the court added that the Retirement Act covered people who did not work for the railroads at the time it was passed—those who had been fired for poor work or had left the railroads to work for other employers. Therefore, it "constitutes a naked appropriation of private property upon the basis of transactions with which the owners of the property were never connected."

RULINGS ON THE SOCIAL SECURITY ACT

New Dealers feared that the Supreme Court's ruling on the Railroad Retirement Act meant that a similar fate awaited Social Security. After all, it also involved a contribution by employees and employers to a compulsory retirement and pension system. As Secretary of Labor Frances Perkins was working on the proposed legislation, she went to a party given by Supreme Court Justice Harlan Fiske Stone. During the party she was talking with Justice Stone, who asked her about the progress being made by her committee on the

Social Security legislation. Perkins said they were afraid the law might be struck down, just like the Railroad Retirement Act. Perkins later recalled, "He looked around to see if anyone was listening" and then told her quietly, "The taxing power, my dear, the taxing power. You can do anything under the taxing power."

As a Supreme Court justice, Stone was not supposed to give advice to a presidential administration on how to write legislation that would be upheld by the court. Nevertheless, he had reminded Perkins that under the U.S. Constitution, Article I, Section 8, "Congress shall have Power To Lay and collect Taxes . . . to pay the Debts and provide for the common Defense and general Welfare of the United States." In the midst of a nationwide depression the Social Security legislation was designed to tax employers and employees to provide for the "general Welfare" of the American people. This clause might outweigh the concerns of the Court over due process.

In 1937 two cases came before the Supreme Court involving the constitutionality of Social Security. These cases were *Helvering* v. *Davis* and *Steward Machine Co.* v. *Davis*. Following close decisions in both cases, the majority ruled in favor of the new law. Delivering the opinion for the majority in *Helvering* v. *Davis*, Justice Benjamin Cardozo stated that Congress had the right to spend money for the "general welfare" of the nation. "The problem is plainly national in area and dimensions," he wrote. "Moreover laws of the separate states cannot deal with it effectively." One issue that arose in the case was that the federal government was using power that should have been reserved for the states. But, as Cardozo added, "States and local governments are often lacking in the resources that are necessary to finance an adequate program of security for the aged." Then he cited evidence to describe the plight of the elderly across the United States. "The evidence is impressive that among industrial workers the younger men and women are preferred over the older. In time of retrenchment [cutbacks and layoffs] the older are commonly the first to go.... The plight of men and women at so low an age as 40 is hard, almost hopeless, when they are driven to seek for reemployment." Thus the Social Security law was upheld by the Supreme Court.

DUE PROCESS AND DISABILITY BENEFITS

More than thirty years after the cases involving the constitutionality of Social Security, another case came before the Supreme Court involving the disability benefits section of the program. In this case George Eldridge had been receiving disability benefits since 1968 because he suffered from severe anxiety and back pain, as well as diabetes. These problems made it impossible for him to work at his job or any other gainful employment. Periodically Eldridge, like other SSDI recipients, was expected to complete a questionnaire assuring the state agency monitoring his disability benefits that he was still unable to work. State agencies regularly check these reports with the doctors treating SSDI recipients. In Eldridge's case, reports obtained by the state agency from his doctor and another medical consultant vowed that he was capable of gainful employment. Therefore in May 1972 the state agency wrote that they were ending his disability payments.

Eldridge wrote back that he had developed a spinal problem that made it impossible for him to work. However, the state agency still decided to stop his payments and informed the Social Security Administration of its decision.

The administration wrote Eldridge that his benefits were ending and that he could appeal his decision within six months. Instead, Eldridge decided to take his case to his district court. His lawyer claimed that his due process rights had been violated under the Fifth Amendment because his benefits had been cut off without a legal hearing.

The district court ruled that Eldridge's due process rights had been violated. The case was eventually appealed by Forrest David Mathews, the secretary of health, education, and welfare, to the U.S. Supreme Court. In a 6 to 2 decision, handed down in 1976, the Supreme Court overruled the lower courts, with Justice Lewis F. Powell Jr., delivering the majority opinion. In *Mathews* v. *Eldridge* Powell wrote that "Due process is flexible, and calls for such procedural protections as the particular situation demands."

Justice Powell pointed out that the state agency had gone through an elaborate procedure before deciding that Eldridge was no longer qualified for SSDI. The agency considered the report of a medical team—a doctor and consultant—and looked at the information on a questionnaire filled out by the worker regarding his health and work restrictions. In addition, Eldridge had been given an opportunity to see the information used by the state agency before making the decision to end his disability benefits. Powell added that "the ultimate additional cost [of any further evaluation process] in terms of money and administrative burden would not be insubstantial." He also added that the "essence of due process is that a person facing a serious loss be given notice of the case and the opportunity to present his side of it." Eldridge had been given due process. Finally, Justice Powell pointed out that a hearing is not required under the Social Security law regarding disability benefits.

Social Security and Student Loans

In another case, which was decided in 2005, the Supreme Court ruled that part of an individual's Social Security benefits can be used to pay off student loan debts. The case involved James Lockhart, a sixty-seven-year-old disabled man living in Seattle, Washington. Lockhart had a student loan debt of $77,000 that he had run up during the 1980s. To help pay off these debts, the federal government reduced Lockhart's $874 monthly Social Security payments. Lockhart appealed the decision to the district court in Washington, which upheld the federal government's position, but the case was appealed to the Supreme Court.

The majority opinion in *Lockhart* v. *United States* was delivered by Justice Sandra Day O'Connor. Lockhart had claimed that the federal Debt Collection Act of 1982 had a ten-year statute of limitations. In other words, after ten years, his student loan debts could not be collected. But O'Connor pointed out that the act was later amended to eliminate any statute of limitations on certain kinds of loans, such as student loans. She added that under normal circumstances the law forbids an individual's Social Security benefits to be taken for the payment of debts. But the amendments to the Debt Collection Act stated that "all payment due an individual under...the Social Security Act...shall be subject to offset [payment for debts]. ..." This is generally limited, however, to 15 percent of the Social Security benefit. But as Lockhart's lawyer, Brian Wolfman, put it after the decision, "It means that you can take the Social Security benefits of someone who is 90 years old and living on a small amount of money. The losers are clearly older Social Security beneficiaries."

BENEFITS FOR WIDOWS AND WIDOWERS

The following year, 1977, the Supreme Court decided a case regarding benefits for widows and widowers under the Social Security law. Social Security not only provided retirement benefits for workers but, if they died, continued paying benefits to their widows and widowers. Under the law a widow continued to receive benefits, but a widower had to prove that he was financially dependent on his wife for at least half of his support before receiving any benefits. A widow was not required to prove dependency. This provision went into effect at a time when most workers were men and their spouses were women who did not earn incomes.

When Mrs. Hannah Goldfarb, a secretary in the New York City school system, died in 1968, her husband, Leon, expected to receive survivor benefits. But Leon Goldfarb was not given those benefits by the Social Security Administration because he had no evidence to show he was financially dependent on his deceased wife. Goldfarb took the case to a district court in New York, which agreed that the law discriminated against him. Therefore, he should receive benefits. The decision was challenged by Joseph Califano, the secretary of health, education, and welfare, and the case went to the Supreme Court.

In a close 5 to 4 decision the Supreme Court upheld the decision of the district court. The court ruled in *Califano v. Goldfarb* that Leon Goldfarb's rights had been violated under the Fifth Amendment, which provides equal protection for all citizens under the law. Justice William Brennan wrote that the law as currently written created a "distinction, which results in the efforts of female workers required to pay social security taxes producing less protection for their spouses than is produced by the efforts of male workers [and] is constitutionally forbidden...."

Many of the Supreme Court decisions regarding Social Security have been controversial, and they have divided the nine justices. Nevertheless, the Supreme Court has upheld the legality of Social Security and clarified some of the program's basic provisions.

Phyllis Rule is shown with several of the six medications she must take every day. Rule is among the teachers who filed a lawsuit against the Michigan Public School Employees Retirement System.

CHAPTER SEVEN

Social Security Benefits: Key Problems

Belinda Virgil, age forty-four, of Fayetteville, North Carolina, suffers from severe emphysema, a lung disease, which requires her to receive oxygen from a tank twenty-four hours a day. Since she was unable to work and had been running up high medical bills, Virgil could no longer pay the rent on her apartment and was forced to live part time at a friend's house and part time at her daughter's home. Her application for Social Security Disability Insurance (SSDI) was initially turned down, and she appealed that decision. "I've got no money for Christmas," she told *New York Times* reporter Erik Eckholm. "I move from house to house, and I'm getting really depressed."

Mark Wild had suffered from diabetes since he was nineteen. Many people have mild cases of diabetes that allow them to continue working. But Wild's illness became so bad that he had to enter a hospital. Although he tried to hold down a job as a cook and a waiter and even enrolled in culinary school,

Wild could only work for short periods before his disability forced him to quit. His application for SSDI was turned down by the Social Security Administration. While appealing the decision, huge medical bills piled up for his family. Finally, in 2006, his mother was telephoned by the family's lawyer and told that the appeal had been approved and that her son would start receiving disability benefits.

But Wild had become so depressed about being turned down for SSDI and the fear that his appeal would be rejected that he killed himself before his appeal had been granted. As Mrs. Wild explained, "No one can say for sure, but we're convinced that his despondency and fear about the disability decision contributed to his death."

According to the Social Security Administration, more than 8 million people were receiving disability benefits in 2007. Each year since 2000 the number of people receiving SSDI has been increasing between 4 and 5 percent. The average amount that an individual receives from SSDI is about $1,000 per month, for a total of about $8 billion. Many people receiving SSDI also qualify for Supplemental Security Income (SSI) because of their low income. The maximum is about $600 per month.

Disabilities are not always easy to detect. For example, someone who is driving a car or mowing a lawn may have a severe emotional problem that prevents him or her from holding down a job. On the other hand, some people who are perfectly capable of being employed fake disabilities to avoid working. They may pretend to have a disability or an illness. Or, after receiving SSDI, they may continue to work without informing the Social Security Administration. Each year, cases of disability fraud are uncovered and prosecuted in court.

In October 2008 the *New York Times* reported that workers on the Long Island Railroad (L.I.R.R.) reported 753 cases of disabling arthritis in 2007, compared to only 32 on another New York railroad. The L.I.R.R. workers hired consultants to help them present their claims, and the same doctors were hired by many of the workers to verify that the claims were real. This eventually led to a federal investigation that discovered many irregularities in the claims and payments.

To prevent fraud and to ensure that those with genuine disabilities are receiving benefits, the Social Security Administration requires that individuals submit to a lengthy process to prove that they are disabled and unable to work. First, individuals claiming disability must meet the Social Security definition of being disabled—that is, they can no longer perform their current jobs or hold down other "gainful" employment. Other employment does not mean any kind of work. For example, a sixty-year-old woman who has worked as an administrative assistant would not be expected to apply for a job requiring heavy physical labor. In addition, the worker must also have a disability that is included on a list of illnesses recognized by the Social Security Administration. These include such things as high blood pressure, serious heart problems, or arthritis that prevent an individual from being employed.

Next, someone applying for SSDI contacts a claims representative at the local Social Security office, who conducts an interview and provides forms that must be filled out by an applicant. The applicant must have proof of identity, a Social Security number, as well as statements from a personal physician supporting the claim of disability, as well as medical records. The local Social Security office then submits the claim to a state agency, usually known as the Disability

Determination Services (DDS). The DDS decides whether to accept the claim or reject it.

The majority of claims are denied by the DDS. The paperwork may not be complete or the illness may not seem fully supported by medical statements from physicians. An individual can then submit the claim for reconsideration, but these are generally denied as well. As a result most disability claimants must go through an appeals process. Generally, they hire an attorney who is experienced in disability claims. The attorney then presents the claim at a hearing in front of an administrative law judge.

According to *New York Times* reporter Erik Eckholm, two-thirds of the cases are won on appeal. Unfortunately, the appeals process can be lengthy. According to Patrick P. O'Carroll Jr., the inspector general of the Social Security Administration, there was a backlog of more than 750,000 cases awaiting a hearing in 2008. And the average waiting period before a case came up for a hearing was 499 days. This was the problem encountered by Belinda Virgil and Mark Wild. The waiting periods are longer in some parts of the United States than in others. According to *USA Today* reporter Richard Wolf, applicants are waiting two and a half years in the Atlanta area. Jeffrey Houston, who was injured on his job when large sheets of glass fell on him, has been waiting more than four years. These long delays place an extra financial burden not only on the applicants but also on the states in which they live. States must provide these workers with welfare payments and Medicaid—health insurance for the poor—because they must wait for a disability claim to be approved.

The Social Security Administration is aware of the problem with disability claims. As Inspector General O'Carroll said in testimony before Congress, there are a variety of reasons for the serious backlog in claims. There are too few staff assistants in some areas of the United States to help administrative law judges handle the cases quickly. In addition, O'Carroll found that hundreds of thousands of cases had fallen through the cracks and were not being tracked or brought up for hearings.

In 2007 the Social Security Administration submitted a plan to Congress that included the hiring of 150 more administrative law judges. Funding was appropriated to increase the number of judges to help reduce the processing time of disability claims.

MEDICARE BENEFITS

More than 44 million people are currently covered by Medicare as part of their Social Security benefits. They rely on Medicare payments to pay hospital and physician costs, as well as other medical expenses, such as prescription drugs and nursing care in their homes. But each year the cost of health care in the United States rises higher, increasing at twice the rate of inflation. People sixty-five and older pay an estimated 25 percent of Medicare costs. But as health-care costs rise, the Social Security cost of living increases don't keep pace, according to Barbara Kennelly, president of the National Committee to Preserve Social Security and Medicare, an organization with 4.6 million members. What's more, premiums for Medicare Part B, which pays doctor bills, have doubled since 2000.

Meanwhile, to deal with rising costs, Congress has raised deductibles and reduced payments to physicians, hospitals, and other health-care providers. As a result, some doctors have refused to take on additional Medicare patients.

What's more, Medicare will not pay for some types of services provided by physicians. While expensive heart surgery is approved, physicians are not fully reimbursed for simply consulting with a patient to figure out a course of treatment for a serious disease. This seriously affects family doctors, sometimes known as general practitioners, as well as other types of physicians.

Dr. Cheryl Woodson, for example, is a geriatrician—a physician who specializes in the health problems of the elderly—who practices in Chicago Heights, Illinois. Dr. Woodson consults with elderly patients and their families "to determine what's wrong with the . . . patient, whether it can be fixed and how to manage things if it can't be, which is often the case. 'I love this. I just love this,'" she told reporter Jane Gross of the *New York Times*. But Medicare reimburses Dr. Woodson for less than 50 percent of her time. "We get paid to do things *to* people [surgical operations]," she says, "not *for* people." As a result, Dr. Gross has decided to keep her current Medicare patients but not to take on any new ones. "If I take new Medicare patients," she said, "I can't keep the door open. . . . You can serve seniors or feed your children."

In 2003 Congress passed the Medicare Modernization Act, which expanded coverage to include prescription drugs. Under the new law the prescription drug plan, Medicare Part D, was run by private insurance companies. The administration of George W. Bush hoped that by privatizing this part of Medicare, competition would ensure that people paid the lowest possible prices for prescription drugs. According to Michael O. Leavitt, secretary of health and human services, "The Medicare drug benefit is saving seniors an average of $1,200 per year."

But problems have arisen in the program. Audits conducted

by the Department of Health and Human Services revealed that some Medicare patients have seen their prescription drug coverage ended by their insurance companies. These patients include those with HIV and AIDS. Others have been forced to accept delays in receiving life-saving drugs because insurance companies have delayed approvals. The Government Accountability Office (GAO), which evaluates federal programs, reported that more than 50 percent of "immediate need complaints" and more than 25 percent of "urgent need complaints" were not handled rapidly.

In addition, according to Nobel Prize–winning economist Paul Krugman, "In the case of the drug benefit, the private drug plans add an extra, costly layer of bureaucracy. Worse yet, they have much less ability to bargain for lower drug prices than government programs like ... the Veterans Health Administration. Reasonable estimates suggest that if Congress had eliminated the middlemen, it could have created a much better drug plan. ..." Medicare might have run the new drug benefit program and negotiated for lower drug prices, according to Krugman. With so many people in the Medicare system, the program could have required drug manufacturers to discount their prices to have their drugs accepted for use by millions of Medicare recipients. But, as Krugman added, Congress voted in 2007 not to give Medicare the power to negotiate lower prices with the drug companies.

What's more, there are holes in the Medicare Part D program. One of these is called the "doughnut hole" by critics of the plan. Under Part D, Medicare beneficiaries have a $250 deductible and then pay 25 percent of prescription costs up to $2,250 per year. Then they pay the full price of prescription drugs until their payments reach $3,600—the so-called doughnut hole. After this amount is reached, they

The Social Security Hole for Female Spouses

When Social Security legislation was passed by Congress in 1935, most workers were men. When a male worker retired, his female spouse received a benefit that was half of what he received. Since that time millions of women have entered the workforce, and the majority of families have two income earners—a husband and wife. Nevertheless, when a woman retires, she must still choose between receiving her own Social Security retirement benefit or half of her husband's benefit. She cannot have both.

have a copay of $2 to $5 for their drugs. This hole increases prescription drug payments for the elderly—many of whom purchase drugs that cost more than $2,250 annually—but saves money for the Medicare program, while drug prices keep going up every year. Krugman claims that Congress "could have created a much better drug plan—one without the notorious 'doughnut hole' . . . at no higher cost" by eliminating the private insurance companies.

As part of the Medicare Modernization Act, Congress also began offering the elderly Medicare Advantage plans. These were designed to add another measure of privatization to the Medicare system and drive down costs. Under the original Medicare program, elderly people had their choice of physicians, but some services—such as eyeglasses—were not covered. The elderly had to pay for these out of their own pockets or purchase medigap insurance plans that covered these health-care services.

Senior citizens who choose a Medicare Advantage plan can join a private health maintenance organization (HMO). The HMOs are required to provide all the coverage available under Medicare Part A and Part B, as well as additional coverage for items such as eyeglasses. But, while the HMOs may offer additional coverage, they generally limit the doctors or hospitals that elderly patients can use. The providers must be in the HMO network of doctors and hospitals.

Retirees can also open Medicare Medical Savings Accounts, begun in 2007, that are run by private insurers. Each person with an account receives an annual tax-free deposit from the insurer. Under one plan the deposit from the insurer is $1,300, which can be used to pay for all medical costs up to an annual deductible of $3,000. Deductibles can be as high as $10,500. Some of the deposits can also be used to pay

Social Security Fraud

Social Security numbers are not only necessary to give people access to a wide range of Social Security benefits, they are also used as a primary source of identification. According to Randy Lively, president and CEO of American Financial Services Association, "The Social Security Number provides a unique identifier that accompanies most consumers from cradle to grave. The number remains a constant in a world where people's names and addresses are constantly changing." As a result, individuals are asked to include their Social Security numbers on such documents as financial forms, credit records, health forms, employment applications, and student ID information. Yet each year thieves gain access to these numbers. They hack into computer records, steal wallets that contain Social Security cards, and rifle through rubbish in which Social Security information might have been discarded on old health forms or credit records. This leads to rampant identity theft, enabling thieves to use Social Security numbers to obtain access to bank accounts, credit card information, and other data.

The Medicare system has flaws as well as benefits. Fraud has become an increasing problem in recent years. Here, federal agents bring suspects in for questioning in a major Medicare fraud sting.

for nonmedical expenses, such as food, but a tax must be paid on the money used for these purposes. The savings accounts benefit those people who accept a high deductible—believing that they will not have high medical costs—or people who can afford to pay for their health care. Supporters also "claim health savings accounts will encourage people to more closely monitor health-care spending and bring down medical costs," wrote *Mother Jones* reporter Michael Scherer. "Critics call the accounts a tax shelter that will benefit the wealthy and draw young, healthy workers out of the health-care plans, potentially doubling the cost of insurance for everyone else."

For example, after Hurricane Katrina struck New Orleans in 2005, the Federal Emergency Management Agency paid millions of dollars to people using false Social Security numbers. Some lawmakers propose that victims of Social Security number fraud should be allowed to obtain different numbers and have their old ones removed from the system. In addition, people are cautioned not to carry their Social Security card with them, where it can be easily stolen by thieves. Finally, they should make sure that any online credit accounts are protected by personal identification numbers (PIN) and passwords. These should be changed regularly.

CHAPTER EIGHT

The Future of Social Security

In August 2005, on the seventieth anniversary of Social Security, President George W. Bush said, "Social Security has been a vital program and helped millions of America's seniors in retirement. The Social Security system is sound for today's seniors, but there is a hole in the safety net for younger workers. On this seventieth anniversary, we renew our commitment to save and strengthen Social Security for our children and grandchildren, and keep the promise of Social Security for future generations."

When President Bush referred to "a hole in the safety net," he was describing a variety of problems that may weaken the Social Security system in the future. One of these problems is the great number of people who began retiring at age sixty-two in 2008. These workers are part of America's baby boom, people who were born between 1946 and 1964. During that period the average number of births per woman reached a peak of 3.7. The baby boom ended during the

President George W. Bush toured the nation to promote the privatization of Social Security, but, in the end, benefits remained under federal control.

1960s because more and more women entered the workforce and had fewer children. The average number of births per woman declined to a low of 1.7 in 1976 and has ranged from 1.82 to 2.07 ever since.

Between 1946 and 1964 approximately 79 million people were born. Those born in 1946 turned sixty-two in 2008, and some of them retired, thus receiving reduced Social Security benefits. In 2011 these same people will reach age sixty-five and will qualify for Medicare. And a year later they will begin retiring with full Social Security benefits. The average annual benefit for a retired person was more than $27,000 in 2008, an increase of 24 percent since 2000 as a result of cost-of-living adjustments. And benefits are expected to continue increasing during the twenty-first century. Retirees are also expected to live longer than they do today, increasing the total benefits paid out even more.

By 2030 approximately 84 million people will be receiving Social Security benefits, an increase of 34 million retirees over 2007. Almost 40 percent of all the income retirees receive comes from Social Security checks. Social Security makes up more than half the income of 66 percent of retired Americans, and all of the income for 20 percent of them.

Nevertheless, providing this income is becoming increasingly difficult. When the system began paying retiree benefits in 1940, only a small number of people received Social Security checks. Large groups of workers were not yet covered by the program, and those who were covered received very small checks.

In the 1940s there were forty-two workers paying Social Security taxes to support each retiree. The ratio of workers to retirees gradually declined as more and more people who had paid into the system retired and began receiving benefits. As the great number of baby boomers retire, beginning in 2009, there will be only three workers paying taxes to support each retiree. (Following the baby boom, birth rates declined, so there were fewer people to enter the workforce once the children born in the late 1960s became of age.) By 2030 there will be only two workers paying taxes to support each retiree. As a result, the financial future of Social Security appears to be very much in doubt.

Each year the trustees of the Social Security and Medicare trust funds issue a report about the status of these programs. These trustees include the secretary of the treasury, the secretary of health and human services, the secretary of labor, and the commissioner of Social Security. In 2008 the trustees said in their report, "The financial condition of the Social Security and Medicare programs remains problematic. Projected long run program costs are not sustainable under current financing arrangements." The trustees' report looked at the amount of money being collected in Social Security payroll taxes each year as well as the size of the trust funds. The trust fund ratio is the amount of benefits paid in Social Security each year compared to the money in the funds. A trust fund ratio of 100 percent or more is considered adequate to sustain the program, according to the trustees. That is, the money in the funds should be enough to cover benefits for a single year. This means that if payroll taxes are too small to pay for all benefits—as part of the pay-as-you-go Social Security program—the trust funds can cover the rest. If a deficit continues for several years, the trust funds will make up the difference until Congress acts to increase payroll taxes.

According to the 2009 trustees report, the trust funds are adequate to cover a year of benefits until 2014. But at that time they begin to fall short. In 2016 payroll taxes will no longer be sufficient to pay Social Security benefits, and the program must dip into the trust funds to make up the difference. By 2037 the trust funds will run out, and payroll taxes will cover only 75 percent of the benefits that newly retired workers are supposed to receive.

To deal with the funding problem, the trustees suggested that payroll-tax revenues be increased from 12.4 percent to 14.1 percent, or benefits be reduced by 12 percent, or a combination of a smaller increase in payroll taxes combined with a smaller reduction in benefits to improve the financing of Social Security. However, a reduction in benefits would have a major impact on those retirees who depend on Social Security for 50 percent or more of their income. An increase in payroll taxes would be especially difficult for low- and middle-income workers who would have less money in their paychecks and face a more difficult task when paying their bills.

OTHER SOLUTIONS TO THE PROBLEM

In addition to raising taxes or lowering benefits, other proposals have been made to deal with Social Security's financial problems. After he was reelected in 2004, President George W. Bush announced that he had made the reform of Social Security a high priority for his administration. Bush was considering a plan proposed by Robert Pozen, chairman of MFS Investment Management and a former head of Fidelity Investments, a large financial services and investment firm.

Pozen's plan included voluntary investment accounts for workers. These would enable workers to put 2 percent of their payroll taxes—a maximum of $3,000—into an investment program. The money would be invested into a combination of stock mutual funds, corporate bond funds, and treasury bond funds rather than going into the Social Security Trust Funds. The stock and corporate bond funds would be invested in a variety of conservative stocks and bonds. The portfolio of stocks and bonds would be managed by private investment firms hired by the federal government. As the Consumer Price Index (CPI), or cost of living, increased, workers could invest a greater amount of money.

Those who opposed privatization of Social Security argued that such a plan would saddle older Americans with benefit cuts, increased risk, and economic instability.

Pozen claimed that a worker could realize an average return from such an investment of 4.8 percent based on market performance over the past decades. Currently, the average return from money in the Social Security Trust Funds invested in treasury bonds is about 1.5 percent. According to Pozen's plan, the money that was placed in the investment accounts by individual workers would be subtracted from payroll taxes paid to the government. In addition, the amount paid into the investment account would be subtracted from Social Security benefits after retirement. On retirement a worker would receive an income from the amount in the investment account. A worker who wanted to open an investment account would, therefore, be gambling that he or she could make more from investing in stock and bond mutual funds than in the treasury bonds.

In addition, Pozen's plan called for a different method of indexing Social Security benefits. At that time a worker received an amount that was based on average wages, indexed to inflation, at retirement. That amount increased based on the rise in the CPI. Wages, on average, rise faster than the CPI, yielding a greater amount upon retirement than a benefit based on CPI. Pozen proposed to change this formula, basing the benefit at retirement for higher-income workers on CPI, beginning in 2012. Workers with incomes under $25,000 would continue to have their initial retirement benefit based on wage indexing.

According to Pozen's plan, retired workers with average earnings of more than $25,000 would have their benefits reduced by 16 percent. Pozen's plan would cut the Social Security budget deficit by about 50 percent, wrote *Consumer Reports*, but would not entirely eliminate it.

According to former congressman and housing secretary Jack Kemp, these voluntary investment accounts would have another benefit. At present the federal government spends the surplus in the Social Security Trust Funds on other projects, promising to pay back the money when the trust funds need it to pay retirement benefits. The Pozen plan would reduce this practice by putting some of the money into individual accounts. The federal government would no longer have as much money in the trust funds to finance projects that it couldn't afford to pay for with the taxes it collects. In addition, according to Kemp, workers would make more money on their payroll taxes invested in stock and bond funds and have greater retirement benefits.

In his article "The Anatomy of Social Security and Medicare," Edgar Browning, a professor of economics at Texas A&M University, supported the idea of investment accounts. Browning pointed out that since 1926, investments in the stock market averaged a 6.9-percent annual return, increasing to 7.1 percent since World War II. While admitting that stocks may be a risky investment, Browning added that some investors prefer corporate bonds. Buying a corporate bond means loaning a corporation money that it agrees to pay back, plus interest. Bonds have generally averaged about a 4-percent return (in interest) in addition to the original investment. Social Security, on the other hand, which uses the money from the trust funds to buy treasury bonds, has only about a 1.5-percent return. Therefore, the trust funds grow very slowly, making it more difficult to pay the benefits for all the workers who retire. Workers could do much better, according to Browning, by investing some of their money in stock and bond mutual funds. They could also increase their retirement income instead of having it reduced by declining Social Security benefits.

Browning pointed out that under his plan, a worker would be required to contribute a fixed amount to a private investment plan each year, which would be deducted from payroll taxes. Once he or she retired, that money would be converted to a pension, with the worker receiving a fixed amount each year. For example, if the amount invested were $1,200 per year, at an average interest rate of 5.5 percent, each worker would have saved $237,000 by retirement at age sixty-six. At 5.5 percent that pension would provide the worker with more than $15,000 per year. This is more than the majority of workers currently receive under Social Security, according to Browning.

However, as Browning readily admitted, the $1,200 deduction from an employee's payroll taxes would mean that less money was available to pay benefits to current retirees. In addition, those workers who were near retirement might be hurt because they had very little time to pay into the private accounts. But, according to Browning, these are the "transition costs" of changing the present system.

Opponents of the Browning plan point out that some workers will not want private accounts. They have little interest in the stock and bond markets and don't want to tell the financial company managing the investment account which mutual funds to invest in. Some of those who do like the idea of private investment accounts may lack the knowledge to make a sound investment. As a result, they could end up doing far worse and receiving a far smaller benefit than they might have received under the traditional Social Security system. The rapid decline in the world stock markets in 2008 indicated how risky investing in stocks and bonds can be.

Some Democrats have supported another plan for dealing with the financial problems. It was proposed by Peter Diamond, a professor at the Massachusetts Institute of Technology, and Peter Orszag of the Brookings Institution, a Washington research organization. The Diamond-Orszag plan calls for an increase in payroll taxes from 12.4 percent to 14.2 percent by 2055. In addition, the amount of wages subject to the payroll tax would increase. And the amount that a worker earned over the wage cap—currently $112,000— would be taxed at 3 percent. In addition, the plan calls for a reduction in benefits by as much as 8.6 percent for younger workers, those who are now twenty-five and under, who still have many years to save and invest before retirement.

In 2006 Democrats in Congress stopped any attempt by the Bush administration to change Social Security. The financial problems continued, leading the 2007 trustees report to warn that Social Security would be unable to pay full benefits to retirees in the years ahead.

MEDICARE FINANCIAL PROBLEMS

In their report the trustees added that Medicare and disability insurance faced even more serious problems than Social Security. "Medicare's financial difficulties come sooner—and are much more severe—than those confronting Social Security." One of the primary reasons is the quickly rising cost of health care, which is increasing faster than salaries, and faster than the payroll taxes paid on them, according to the trustees.

According to the *New York Times*, the United States spends more on health care than any other nation in the world. And these costs have almost doubled since 2000. To pay for hospital costs, Medicare Part A relies on payroll taxes from workers, as well as the money collected in the Hospital Insurance Trust Fund. In 2008, 44.1 million workers were receiving Medicare benefits. According to the 2008 trustees' report that fund will run out of money in 2019. This will leave only the taxes collected from workers to pay for Medicare Part A, and these will be sufficient to fund only 78 percent of medical benefits under the program.

Medicare Part B pays for physicians. The trust fund covering this part of the program is in sound financial condition because it raises premiums each year to pay for health-care costs. For example, those enrolled in Part B paid $96.40 per month in 2008, and if their incomes were greater than $82,000 per year, they were charged even more.

To deal with higher health-care costs, Medicare must charge higher premiums while lowering benefits, with higher copayments made by retirees and higher deductibles. This will be especially difficult for many elderly retirees who already spend 22 percent of their income on Medicare premiums and out-of-pocket expenses and will spend as much as 30 percent of their income by 2025, according to Dr. Karen Davis and Dr. Sara Collins, members of the Commonwealth Fund, a private foundation committed to improving the Health Care fund. They add that the elderly will be spending as much as $100,000 each year for health-care costs, and that figure could increase to more than $300,000 if they live into their nineties.

A survey by the Commonwealth Fund found that 70 percent of adults between the ages of fifty and seventy favored a Medicare health account, similar to the Social Security private investment accounts. Workers would be given the option of investing as much as 3 percent of their salaries— over and above payroll taxes—in government bonds and using the interest earned on these bonds to pay for the extra costs of health care when they retire. In addition, Medicare could also strive to reduce health-care costs. As Davis and Collins wrote, "Medicare payment could . . . provide bonuses to hospitals, physicians, and other health care providers who achieve high levels of quality and efficiency. . . ." Medicare could also provide a financial reward to patients who use hospitals and physicians who "rank high on quality and low on total cost of care."

Perhaps the only way to improve Medicare's financial problems is to reform the entire health-care system. Various reforms were discussed during the 2008 presidential election by Republican candidate John McCain and Democratic candidate Barack Obama. They have discussed plans to permit Medicare to negotiate prices with the pharmaceutical companies that supply drugs; to spend more money on preventive medicine, which is cheaper than treating medical problems when they become severe; and to share more information between hospitals so they can learn from each other about the quickest and most cost-effective methods of treating illnesses. President Obama spent part of his first year in office reexamining Medicare costs and financing, as well as also taking a preliminary look at Social Security.

DISABILITY AND MEDICAID

In addition to the financial problems with Medicare and Social Security, disability insurance also faces serious challenges in the years ahead. In 2007 approximately $8 billion was paid in disability benefits under the Social Security Disability Insurance program. This was an average of almost $1,000 monthly to about 8 million people. However, according to the U.S. Government Accountability Office (GAO), which monitors federal government operations, the Disability Trust Fund could run out of money by 2026.

In a report issued in 2007, the GAO stated that proposals to deal with the financial challenges facing disability insurance are similar to those that have been considered for fixing Social Security. These include new indexing measures. At the present time disability benefits are indexed to increases

President Obama has committed himself to reexamining the financing of Social Security as well as to extending medical insurance to the uninsured and curbing Medicare fraud and other systemic problems.

in wages. One proposal is to index them to the increase in the cost of living. According to the GAO, this would lead to a reduction of as much as 30 percent in disability benefits for many people now receiving them. Instead, the GAO proposed a graduated form of price indexing, which meant that low-income workers would still have their benefits based on wages rather than prices. This affects far fewer of those people receiving SSDI.

Like disability and Medicare, Medicaid is also facing a financial crisis. According to the Kaiser Family Foundation, a nonprofit organization that issues regular reports on health-care issues, more than 52 million people are enrolled in Medicaid, at a cost of approximately $300 billion. About 57 percent of the funding comes from the federal government, while the rest comes from the individual states. The Centers for Medicare and Medicaid Services oversee Medicaid, but each state runs its own program.

To control increasing health-care costs, the federal government has been cutting back on Medicaid payments. This has put greater pressure on individual states to pay Medicaid costs. But as these costs have risen by 9 to 12 percent yearly, states have been increasingly hard pressed to make up the difference. In 2005 *Business Week* reported, "Already, states are scrambling to cut costs . . . 47 states are cutting or freezing payments to doctors and hospitals this year; 43 are lowering [what they will pay for] drug costs . . . 9 are cutting benefits, and 9 are increasing patient copayments."

In California the state government eliminated more than $500 million from the Medicaid budget because of a budget crisis in 2008. This came during a nationwide economic downturn that put many people out of work. As a result they lost their incomes, no longer received health insurance coverage at their jobs, and had to turn to Medicaid.

The financial problems affecting Social Security could never have been envisioned in 1935 by the originators of the program. At that time Social Security was a program designed to provide only a small income supplement to those who had retired. Since that time the scope of the Social Security programs have grown, encompassing health care and disability as well as retirement income. Over the next few decades there will be a great number of people retiring, combined with ever-rising costs of health care.

The day after President Obama signed a comprehensive health care bill into law, the *New York Times* reported on an unanticipated drop in payroll taxes to support social security. The Congressional Budget Office reported that, in 2010, rather than 2016, as had been expected, the Social Security system would pay out more in benefits than it would take in through payroll taxes. This was believed to be the result of high unemployment and a troubled economy.

Moving forward, Social Security must balance the need to provide adequate benefits with the necessity of ensuring adequate financing to safeguard the system. As a result, the Social Security system may undergo drastic changes.

From Bill to Law

For a proposal to become a federal law, it must go through many steps:

In Congress:

1. A bill is proposed by a citizen, a legislator, the president, or another interested party. Most bills originate in the House and then are considered in the Senate.

2. A representative submits the bill to the House (the first reading). A senator submits it to the Senate. The person (or people) who introduces the bill is its main sponsor. Other lawmakers can become sponsors to show support for the bill. Each bill is read three times before the House or the Senate.

3. The bill is assigned a number and referred to the committee(s) and subcommittee(s) dealing with the topic. Each committee adopts its own rules, following guidelines of the House and the Senate. The committee chair controls scheduling for the bill.

4. The committees hold hearings if the bill is controversial or complex. Experts and members of the public may testify. Congress may compel witnesses to testify if they do not do so voluntarily.

5. The committee reviews the bill, discusses it, adds amendments, and makes other changes it deems necessary during markup sessions.

6. The committee votes on whether to support the bill, oppose it, or take no action on it and issues a report on its findings and recommendations.

7. A bill that receives a favorable committee report goes to the Rules Committee to be scheduled for consideration by the full House or Senate.

8. If the committee delays a bill or if the Rules Committee fails to schedule it, House members can sign a discharge motion and call for a vote on the matter. If a majority votes to release the bill from committee, it is scheduled on the calendar as any other bill would be. Senators may vote to discharge the bill from a committee as well. More commonly, though, a senator will add the bill as an amendment to an unrelated bill in order to get it past the committee blocking it. Or a senator can request that a bill be put directly on the Senate calendar, where it will be scheduled for debate. House and Senate members can also vote to suspend the rules and vote directly on a bill. Bills passed in this way must receive support from two-thirds of those voting.

9. Members of both houses debate the bill. In the House, a chairperson moderates the discussion and each speaker's time is limited. Senators can speak on the issue for as long as they wish. Senators who want to block the bill may debate for hours in a tactic known as a filibuster. A three-fifths vote of the Senate is required to stop the filibuster (cloture), and talk on the bill is then limited to one hour per senator.

10. Following the debate, the bill is read section by section (the second reading). Members may propose amendments, which are voted on before the final bill comes up for a vote.

11. The full House and Senate then debate the entire bill and those amendments approved previously. Debate continues until a majority of members vote to "move the previous question" or approve a special resolution forcing a vote.

12. A full quorum—at least 218 members in the House, 51 in the Senate—must be present for a vote to be held. A member may request a formal count of members to ensure a quorum is on hand. Absent members are sought when there is no quorum.

13. Before final passage, opponents are given a last chance to propose amendments that alter the bill; the members vote on them.

14. A bill needs approval from a majority of those voting to pass. Members who do not want to take a stand on the issue may choose to abstain (not vote at all) or merely vote present.

15. If the House passes the bill, it goes on to the Senate. By that time, bills often have more than one hundred amendments attached to them. Occasionally, a Senate bill will go to the House.

16. If the bill passes in the same form in both the House and the Senate, it is sent to the clerk to be recorded.

17. If the Senate and the House version differ, the Senate sends the bill to the House with the request that members approve the changes.

18. If the two houses disagree on the changes, the bill may go to conference, where members appointed by the House and the Senate work out a compromise if possible.

19. The House and the Senate vote on the revised bill agreed to in conference. Further amendments may be added and the process repeated if the Senate and the House version of the bill differ.

20. The bill goes to the president for a signature.

To the President:

1. If the president signs the bill, it becomes law.

2. If the president vetoes the bill, it goes back to Congress, which can override his veto with a two-thirds vote in both houses.

3. If the president takes no action, the bill automatically becomes law after ten days if Congress is still in session.

4. If Congress adjourns and the president has taken no action on the bill within ten days, it does not become law. This is known as a pocket veto.

The time from introduction of the bill to the signing can range from several months to the entire two-year session. If a bill does not win approval during the session, it can be reintroduced in the next Congress, where it will have to go through the whole process again.

Chronology

1929 Great Depression begins.

1932 Franklin D. Roosevelt is elected president.

1935 Social Security is enacted.

1936 Supreme Court upholds constitutionality of Social Security.

1939 Amendments increase Social Security benefits.

1954 Amendments expand Social Security coverage to more workers.

1956 Social Security includes disability benefits.

1965 Medicare and Medicaid become law.

1972 Congress enacts Supplemental Security Income program to help the elderly poor, blind, and disabled.

1975 Supreme Court rules that widows and widowers are entitled to the same survivor benefits under Social Security.

1977 Social Security amendments are passed by Congress.

1983 Presidential commission is formed to provide financial stability to Social Security system.

1980s–1990s Social Security taxes and benefits increase. Supreme Court rules that an individual can lose part of Social Security benefits to pay student loan debts. President George W. Bush proposes voluntary investment accounts to help finance Social Security.

2008 Social Security Board of Trustees calls financing of Social Security "problematic."

Notes

Chapter 1

p. 9, "Brother, Can You Spare a Dime? . . . ": Yip Harburg and Jay Gorney, "Songs of the Great Depression," www.library.csi.cuny.edu/dept/history/lavender/cherries.html (accessed October 15, 2008).

p. 9, "About 25 percent . . .": "Timelines of the Great Depression," www.huppi.com/kangaroo/Timeline.htm (accessed October 15, 2008).

p. 11, "There was a time . . .": Peter Bernstein, "What's Free About Free Enterprise?" *New York Times*, September 28, 2008, 1.

p. 11, "Fewer than 1 percent . . .": Nancy Altman, *The Battle for Social Security*, New York: Wiley, 2005, 22.

p. 11, "In New York, for example . . .": Altman, *The Battle for Social Security,* 27.

p. 12, "I place the security of the men . . .": Franklin D. Roosevelt, "Message to Congress Reviewing the Board Objectives and Accomplishments of the Administration," *Social Security Online*, www.ssa.gov/history/fdrstmts.html#message1 (accessed August 19, 2009).

pp. 12, 14, "I see no reason. . .": Franklin D. Roosevelt, quoted by Frances Perkins, *The Roosevelt I Knew*, New York: Viking, 1946, 282.

p. 14, "A brilliant, sharp-tongued woman . . .": Altman, *The Battle for Social Security,* 41.

p. 14, "As they worked together on the program . . ." Altman, *The Battle for Social Security,* 46–47.

p. 17, "No sooner was the bill . . .": Altman, *The Battle for Social Security,* 27–28.

p. 17, "Under its provisions . . .": Altman, *The Battle for Social Security,* 80–81.

p. 18, "The most prosperous companies . . .": Altman, *The Battle for Social Security,* 75.

Chapter 2

p. 21, "I'll certainly tell you how it strikes me . . .": Cephalus, quoted in Pat Thane, ed., *A History of Old Age*, London: Thames and Hudson, 2005, 14.

p. 22, "repaying the debt...": Cephalus, quoted in Thane, ed., *A History of Old Age*, 44.

p. 22, "For our parents...": Hierocles, quoted in Thane, ed., *A History of Old Age*, 45.

p. 22, "gruel to lick up...": Aristophanes, quoted in Thane, ed., *A History of Old Age*, 45.

p. 22, "Old age will only be respected..." Cicero, quoted in Thane, ed., *A History of Old Age*, 69.

p. 22, "only about 8 percent...": Thane, ed., *A History of Old Age*, 71.

p. 23, "Andrea Gritti...": Thane, ed., *A History of Old Age*, 80–81, 89.

p. 23, "Many poor men and women...": Thane, ed., *A History of Old Age*, 107.

p. 24, "a community was obligated...": Thane, ed., *A History of Old Age*, 178.

p. 24, "old age pensions...": Thane, ed., *A History of Old Age*, 183.

p. 25, "And last of all...": Anne Bradstreet, quoted in Thomas Cole, *The Journey of Life: A Cultural History of Aging in America* New York: Cambridge University Press, 1992, 37.

p. 25, "generally lived long lives...": Cole, *The Journey of Life*, 55.

p. 25, "During the eighteenth century, the authority...": Cole, *The Journey of Life*, 50.

p. 26, "Nothing is more incumbent...": Thomas Jefferson, quoted in Thane, ed., *A History of Old Age*, 214.

p. 26, "Nathaniel Emmons...": Cole, *The Journey of Life*, 58.

p. 26, "Rip's fate...": Cole, *The Journey of Life*, 75.

p. 28, "It is an advantage...": Albert Barnes, quoted in Cole, *The Journey of Life*, 89.

p. 28, "wears out its workers...": E. T. Devine, *Misery and Its Causes*, 125, quoted in Abraham Epstein, *Facing Old Age*, New York: Knopf, 1922, 4.

p. 30, "A man's productive...": Report of the Committee on Economic Security, "The Economic Problems of Old Age, Part II," Washington: U.S. Government Printing Office, 1937, 138.

p. 30, "A study of a Massachusetts...": Nancy Altman, *The Battle for Social Security* New York: Wiley, 2005, 7.

p. 30, "The poorhouse was a fate...": Altman, *The Battle for Social Security*, 7–8.

Chapter 3

p. 31, "Young people have come to wonder...": Franklin Roosevelt, "Presidential Statement Singing the Social Security Act," *Social Security*

Online, www.ssa.gov/history/fdrstmts.html#signing (accessed October 17, 2008).

p. 33, "Approximately 26 million . . .": Nancy Altman, *The Battle for Social Security*, New York: Wiley, 2005, 109, 150; Sylvester Scheiber and John Shoven, *The Real Deal: The History and Future of Social Security*, New Haven: Yale University Press, 1999, 61.

p. 34, "I read it and got interested . . .": Arthur Altmeyer, quoted in Larry DeWitt, "Never Finished a Thing: A Brief Biography of Arthur Joseph Altmeyer—the Man FDR Called 'Mr. Social Security,'" *Social Security Online*, www.ssa.gov/history/bioaja.html (accessed October 17, 2008).

p. 35, "When the public turns to government . . .": Altemeyer, quoted in DeWitt, "Never Finished a Thing."

p. 37, "The Republicans also warned . . .": Scheiber and Shoven, *The Real Deal*, 52–53.

p. 38, "You're *sentenced* . . .": Republican campaign pamphlet, quoted in Scheiber and Shoven, *The Real Deal*, 53–54.

p. 39, "Since 1940 was an election year . . .": Altman, *The Battle for Social Security,* 109, 150; Scheiber and Shoven, *The Real Deal*, 130–133.

p. 40, "For example, the worker . . .": Scheiber and Shoven, *The Real Deal*, 61.

p. 41, "This program is just starting up . . .": Robert Ball quoted in Patricia Sullivan, "Robert M. Ball; 'Spiritual Leader' of Social Security," *Washington Post*, January 23, 2008, B7.

p. 43, "The new law also extended . . .": Scheiber and Shoven, *The Real Deal*, 90.

Chapter 4

p. 45, "Government is an instrument . . .": Arthur Altmeyer, quoted in Larry DeWitt, "Never Finished a Thing: A Brief Biography of Arthur Joseph Altmeyer—the Man FDR Called 'Mr. Social Security,'" *Social Security Online*, www.ssa.gov/history/bioaja.html (accessed October 17, 2008).

p. 46, "That year . . .": Nancy Altman, *The Battle for Social Security*, New York: Wiley, 2005, 181.

p. 48, "might have been . . .": John F. Kennedy, quoted in Altman, *The Battle for Social Security,* 195.

p. 50, "No longer will older Americans. . .": Lyndon Johnson, quoted in Altman, *The Battle for Social Security,* 205.

p. 50, "Meanwhile, payroll taxes . . .": Sylvester Scheiber and John Shoven, *The Real Deal: The History and Future of Social Security*, New Haven: Yale University Press, 1999, 152.

p. 51, "SSI is a federal-state . . .": Joseph Matthews, *Social Security, Medicare and Government Pensions*, Berkeley, CA: Nolo Publishers, 2006, 6/2.

p. 51, "While inflation—the rise in cost . . .": Scheiber and Shoven, *The Real Deal*, 173.

p. 51, "That deficit hit $5.6 billion . . .": Scheiber and Shoven, *The Real Deal*, 174–177.

p. 52, "Nevertheless, the high rate of inflation . . .": Scheiber and Shoven, *The Real Deal*, 184.

p. 52, "Among the early proposals . . .": Altman, *The Battle for Social Security*, 228–231.

pp. 52–53, "Social Security System is teetering . . .": Ronald Reagan, quoted in Altman, *The Battle for Social Security*, 232.

p. 54, "The fifteen-member commission . . .": Scheiber and Shoven, *The Real Deal*, 189.

p. 54, "The Greenspan Commission . . .": Scheiber and Shoven, *The Real Deal*, 191–194.

p. 55, "Meanwhile, Ball offered suggestions . . .": Scheiber and Shoven, *The Real Deal*, 192–193; Altman, *The Battle for Social Security*, 250–252.

Chapter 5

p. 59, "Approximately 49 million people . . .": "Social Security: Evaluating the Structure for Basic Benefits," Washington, D.C.: American Academy of Actuaries, September 2007, 2.

p. 59, "The employee's share is . . .": "Your Social Security Statement," Social Security Administration, August 15, 2008, 3.

p. 60, "Those earning low salaries . . .": Joseph L. Matthews, *Social Security Medicare and Government Pensions*, Berkeley, CA: Nolo, 2002, 1/12–1/13.

p. 61, "In 2009, for example . . .": National Public Radio, "Morning Edition," October 24, 2008.

p. 61, "For example, a man . . .": "Your Social Security Statement," August 15, 2008, 3.

p. 61, "Social Security benefits may also be taxed . . .": Matthews, *Social Security, Medicare and Government Pensions*, 1/13.

pp. 61–62, "Monthly benefits from Social Security . . .": "Social Security: Evaluating the Structure for Basic Benefits," September 2007, 2.

p. 62, "Approximately 10 percent of the elderly . . .": *The World Almanac and Book of Facts*, New York: World Almanac Education Group, 2006, 98.

p. 63, "If a man received $900 . . .": Matthews, *Social Security, Medicare and Government Pensions*, 4/5.

p. 63, "Poverty is a serious problem . . .": Government Accountability Office, "Medicare Part D Low Income Subsidy," *GAO Highlights*, 2007.

p. 63, "The surviving spouse of a worker . . .": Matthews, *Social Security, Medicare and Government Pensions*, 5/7.

p. 64, "For example, a thirty-four-year-old worker . . .": Matthews, *Social Security, Medicare and Government Pensions*, 5/6–5/7.

p. 64, "Each month Social Security . . .": Actuarial Publications, "Selected Data from Social Security's Disability Program," *Social Security Online*, www.ssa.gov/OACT/STATS/dibStat.html (accessed October 24, 2008).

p. 65, "is expected to last . . .": Matthews, *Social Security, Medicare and Government Pensions*, 3/6–3/8.

p. 65, "Approximately 44 million people . . .": Center for Medicare Advocacy, Inc., "Quick Reference Medicare Facts and Statistics," www.medicare advocacy.org/FAQ_QuickStats.htm (accessed October 24, 2008).

p. 66, "Medigap plans cover coinsurance . . .": AARP, "Medigap Plans: Listing by Coverage," www.aarp.org/health/medicare/supplemental/2003-06-02-medigapcharts.html (accessed October 24, 2008).

Chapter 6

p. 73, "A railroad's assets . . .": *Railroad Retirement Board v. Alton Railroad Co.*, 295 U.S. 330 (1935), http://supreme.justia.com/us/295/330 (accessed October 27, 2008).

p. 74, "He looked around . . .": Frances Perkins, quoted in Sylvester Scheiber and John Shoven, *The Real Deal: The History and Future of Social Security*, New Haven: Yale University Press, 1999, 43–44.

p. 74, "The problem is plainly national . . .": Benjamin Cardozo, quoted in *Helvering v. George P. Davis*, 910 U.S. (1936), *Social Security Online*, www. ssa.gov/history/supreme1.html (accessed October 27, 2008).

p. 76, "Due process is flexible . . .": *Mathews v. Eldridge*, 424 U.S. 319 (1976), http://law.jrank.org/pages/12895/Mathews-v-Eldridge.html (accessed October 27, 2008).

p. 76, "the ultimate additional cost . . .": *Mathews v. Eldridge*, 424 U.S. 319 (1976).

p. 77, "all payment due an individual . . .": *Lockhart v. United States et al.*, 546 U.S. (2005), http://supreme.justia.com/us/546/04-881/ (accessed August 20, 2008).

p. 77, "It means . . .": Bruce Wolfman, quoted in "Supreme Court Says Feds Can Grab Social Security to Pay Old Student Loans," *Senior Journal.com*, http://seniorjournal.com/NEWS/SocialSecurity/5-12-08-SS-Student Loans.htm (accessed October 27, 2008).

p. 78, "distinction, which results . . .": *Califano* v. *Goldfarb*, 430 U.S. 199 (1977), www.law.cornell.edu/supct/html/historics/USSC_CR_0430_0199 _ZS.html (accessed October 27, 2008).

Chapter 7

p. 81, "I've got no money . . .": Belinda Virgil, quoted in Erik Eckholm, "Disability Cases Last Longer as Backlog Rises," *The New York Times*, December 10, 2007, www.nytimes.com/2007/12/10/disability.html?_r=1&oref= slogin&pagewanted=print (accessed October 30, 2008).

p. 82, "No one can say for sure . . .": Mrs. Wild, quoted in Eckholm, "Disability Cases Last Longer as Backlog Rises," December 10, 2007.

p. 82, "According to the Social Security Administration . . .": Actuarial Publications, "Selected Data from Social Security's Disability Program," *Social Security Online*, www.ssa.gov/OACT/STATS/dibStat.html (accessed October 24, 2008); Allison Bell, "For Many Aging Breadwinners, SSDI Is Just Another Acronym," *National Underwriter: Life and Health*, June 16, 2008.

p. 83, "In October 2008 . . .": Walt Bogdanich, "Doctors and Advisers Eased Path for L.I.I.R. Disability Claims," *New York Times*, October 27, 2008.

p. 84, "two thirds of the cases . . .": Eckholm, "Disability Cases Last Longer as Backlog Rises," December 10, 2007.

p. 84, "there was a backlog . . .": Patrick P. O'Carroll, House Committee on Appropriations, *Social Security Backlog Congressional Testimony,* February 28, 2008, www.ebscohost.com (accessed October 16, 2008).

p. 84, "Applicants are waiting two and a half years . . .": Richard Wolf, "Disability Delays Can Lead to Personal Havoc," *USA Today*, July 30, 2007.

pp. 84–85, "As Inspector General O'Carroll said in testimony . . .": O'Carroll, *Social Security Backlog Congressional Testimony*, February 28, 2008.

p. 85, "People sixty-five and older pay . . .": William Welch, "Medicare: The Next Riddle for the Ages," *USA Today*, March 16, 2005.

p. 85, "but as health-care costs rise . . .": Barbara Kennelly, House Energy and Commerce Committee, "Medicare Physician Payment System," Congressional Testimony, November 17, 2005, www.ebscohost.com (accessed October 16, 2008).

p. 86, "to determine what's wrong . . .": Jane Gross, "When Medicare Falls Short," *New York Times*, October 16, 2008.

p. 86, "The Medicare drug . . .": Michael O. Leavitt, quoted in Robert Pear, "Medicare Audits Show Problems in Private Plans," *New York Times*, October 7, 2007.

p. 87, "The Government Accountability . . .": "New GAO Report Reveals Continuing Problems Resolving Medicare Drug Plan Complaints and Grievances," *House Oversight and Government Reform Committee*, July 28, 2008, http://oversight.house.gov/story.asp?id=2124 (accessed October 16, 2009).

p. 87, "In the case of the drug benefit . . .": Paul Krugman, "The Plot Against Medicare," *New York Times*, April 20, 2007.

p. 87, "the so-called doughnut hole . . .": Anna Bates, "Why Bush's Medicare Drug Plan Is Just Plain Wrong," *Political Affairs Magazine*, February 27, 2007, www.politicalaffairs.net/article/view/4923/1/244/?Printable Version=enabled (accessed October 30, 2008).

p. 89, "could have created . . .": Krugman, "The Plot Against Medicare," April 20, 2007.

p. 91, "The Social Security Number provides . . .": Randy Lively Jr., "Social Security Numbers: Privacy v. Benefits," Congressional Testimony, May 11, 2006, www.ebscohost.com (accessed October 16, 2008).

p. 92, "claim health savings accounts . . .": Michael Scherer, "Medicare's Hidden Bonanza," *Mother Jones*, March/April 2004, www.motherjones.com/news/outfront/2004/03/02_401.html (accessed October 30, 2008).

p. 92, "After Hurricane Katrina struck . . .": Kevin McCoy, "Safeguards Too Weak to Catch Fraud," *USA Today*, February 13, 2006.

Chapter 8

p. 93, "Social Security has been a vital program . . .": George Bush, "President's Statement on the 70th Anniversary of Social Security," *The White House: President George W. Bush*, www.whitehouse.gov/news/releases/2005/08/print/20050814-2.html (accessed November 3, 2008).

p. 93, "During that period . . .": Edgar K. Browning, "The Anatomy of Social Security and Medicare," *The Independent Review*, Summer 2008, 17.

p. 94, "Between 1946 and 1964 . . .": Dennis Cauchon, "Senior Benefit Costs up 24%," *USA Today*, February 14, 2008.

p. 95, "Almost 40 percent of all the income received . . .": Kevin McCormally, "Social Security's Future . . . and Yours," *Kiplinger's Personal Finance*, Fall 2005, 22.

p. 95, "In the 1940s there were forty-two workers . . .": Richard Wolf, "Social Security Hits First Wave of Boomers," *USA Today*, October 9, 2007.

p. 96, "In 2008 the trustees said . . .": "Status of the Social Security and Medicare Programs," *Trustees Report Summary*, 2008, www.ssa.gov/OACT/TRSUM/index.html (accessed November 3, 2008).

p. 96, "The financial condition . . .": "Status of the Social Security and Medicare Programs," 2008.

p. 96, "To deal with the funding problem . . .": "Status of the Social Security and Medicare Programs," 2008.

p. 98, "Pozen claimed that . . .": "Social Security: What's On the Table," *Consumer Reports*, August 2005, 46.

p. 99, "In addition, Pozen's plan . . .":,"Social Security: What's On the Table," 46.

p. 99, "Pozen's plan would . . .":, "Social Security: What's On the Table," 48.

p. 100, "The federal government . . .": Jack Kemp, "Bush Gets Boost on Social Security Reform," *Human Events*, July 4, 2005, 1–2.

p. 100, "In his article . . .": Browning, "The Anatomy of Social Security and Medicare," 5–25.

p. 100, "Browning pointed out . . .": Browning, "The Anatomy of Social Security and Medicare," 12.

p. 101, "These are the 'transition costs' . . .": Browning, "The Anatomy of Social Security and Medicare," 25.

p. 101, "Opponents of the Browning plan . . .": Jack M. Marco, "Personal Accounts Could Add New Risk," *Pensions and Investments*, June 27, 2005.

p. 101, "The Diamond-Orzag plan calls for . . .": "Social Security: What's On the Table,"47.

p. 102, "Medicare's financial difficulties come sooner . . .": "Status of the Social Security and Medicare Programs," 2008.

p. 102, "the United States spends more on health care . . .": Billy Beane, Newt Gingrich, John Kerry, "How to Take American Health Care from Worst to First," *New York Times*, October 24, 2008.

p. 102, "that fund will run out of money . . .": "Status of the Social Security and Medicare Programs," 2008.

p. 103, "This will be especially difficult for many elderly retirees . . .": Karen Davis and Sara Collins, "Medicare at Forty," *Health Care Financing Review*, Winter 2005–2006, 54.

p. 103, "A survey by the Commonwealth Fund . . .": Davis and Collins, "Medicare at Forty," 54.

p. 103, "Medicare payment could . . .": Davis and Collins, "Medicare at Forty," 54.

p. 104, "They have discussed . . .": "Age Shall Not Wither Them," *The Economist*, November 1, 2008, 30.

p. 104, "In addition to the financial problems . . .": Allison Bell, "For Many Aging Breadwinners, SSDI Is Just Another Acronym," *National Underwriter, Life and Health*, June 16, 2008.

p. 104, "In a report issued in 2007, the GAO stated . . .": Government Accountability Office, "Social Security Reform: Issues for Disability and Dependent Benefits," *GAO Highlights*, 2007.

p. 106, "In 2005 *Business Week* reported . . .": Joe Auciello, "The Bush Agenda: No Aid for Medicaid," *Labor Standard*, www.laborstandard.org/New_Postings/Medicaid.htm (accessed November 3, 2008).

p. 106, "In California the state government . . .": "Medicaid in Crisis as Bush Administration Tries to Shift Billions in Cost to States," *Senior Journal*, http://seniorjournal.com/NEWS/Medicaid/2008-02-21-Medicaid inCrisis.htm (accessed November 3, 2008).

All websites available as of August 19, 2009.

Further Information

BOOKS

Altman, Nancy. *The Battle for Social Security*. New York: John Wiley, 2005.

Thane, Pat, ed. *A History of Old Age*. London: Thames and Hudson, 2005.

Worth, Richard. *Workers' Rights*. New York: Marshall Cavendish, 2008.

WEBSITES

Social Security Online
www.ssa.gov

U.S. Government Documents
www.ourdocuments.gov

U.S. Supreme Court Cases and Decisions
http://supreme.justia.com

Bibliography

BOOKS

Altman, Nancy. *The Battle for Social Security*. New York: Wiley, 2005.

Cole, Thomas. *The Journey of Life: A Cultural History of Aging in America*. New York: Cambridge University Press, 1992.

Matthews, Joseph. *Social Security, Medicare and Government Pensions*. Berkeley, CA: Nolo Press, 2006.

Schieber, Sylvester and John Shoven. *The Real Deal: The History and Future of Social Security*. New Haven, Yale University Press, 1999.

Thane, Pat, ed. *A History of Old Age*. London: Thames and Hudson, 2005.

WEBSITES

The Board of Trustees, Federal Old-Age and Survivors Insurance and Federal Disability Insurance Trust Funds. *2009 Annual Report*, Washington, DC: U.S. Government Printing Office, May 12, 2009.
www.ssa.gov/OACT/TR/2009/tr09.pdf
(accessed August 13, 2009).

Center for Medicare Advocacy
www.medicareadvocacy.org

Cornell University Law School, "Supreme Court Collection."
www.law.cornell.edu/supct/html

Department of Health and Human Services. *The 2009 HHS Poverty Guidelines.* Washington, DC: U.S. Government Printing Office, February 27, 2009.
www.aspe.hhs.gov/POVERTY/09poverty.shtml
(accessed August 13, 2009)

Law Library, American Law and Legal Information
http://law.jrank.org

Social Security Online, www.ssa.gov
(accessed August 19, 2009)

All websites available as of August 19, 2009.

Index

Page numbers in **boldface** are illustrations, tables, and charts.

About the Author

RICHARD WORTH is the author of more than fifty books, including books on history, politics, current events, and biographies. His most recent books for Marshall Cavendish Benchmark were *Legal Gambling: Winner or Loser?* in the Controversy! series and *1950s to 1960s* and *1970s to 1980s* in our Hispanic America series. He lives in Connecticut.